A CUP OF COMFORT® for Christmas

Stories that celebrate
the warmth, joy, and
wonder of the holiday

Edited by Colleen Sell

adamsmedia
Avon, Massachusetts

In memory of Frank Joseph Baum and in celebration of Patrick Sell,
who've made all the Swell family Christmases bright.

Published by
Adams Media, an F+W Publications Company
57 Littlefield Street, Avon, MA 02322. U.S.A.
www.adamsmedia.com and *www.cupofcomfort.com*
ISBN 10: 1-59869-658-0
ISBN 13: 978-1-59869-658-5

Printed in the United States of America.

J I H G F E D C B A

Library of Congress Cataloging-in-Publication Data
A cup of comfort for Christmas / edited by Colleen Sell.
p.   cm.
1. Christmas. I. Sell, Colleen.
GT4985.C75 2003
394.2663--dc21
2003011081

This publication is designed to provide accurate and authoritative information
with regard to the subject matter covered. It is sold with the understanding that
the publisher is not engaged in rendering legal, accounting, or other professional
advice. If legal advice or other expert assistance is required, the services of a
competent professional person should be sought.
   —From a *Declaration of Principles* jointly adopted by a Committee of the
American Bar Association and a Committee of Publishers and Associations

Many of the designations used by manufacturers and sellers to distinguish their
products are claimed as trademarks. Where those designations appear in this book
and Adams Media was aware of a trademark claim, the designations have been
printed with initial capital letters.

This book is available at quantity discounts for bulk purchases.
For information, call 1-800-289-0963.

Acknowledgments

While writing and editing are solo acts, publishing is a coordinated concert of many in which each performer plays a vital part. *A Cup of Comfort for Christmas* absolutely sings, and it does so because of the talents and efforts and cooperation and patience and generosity of the team at Adams Media and of all the authors who've contributed their terrific stories to this collection. I give a standing ovation and a rousing round of applause to each and every one of you.

A special thanks and an enormous bouquet of posies go to Kate Epstein and Laura MacLaughlin, my co-conductors in this joyous composition. Please take a bow, ladies.

I am most grateful to Bob Adams for allowing me the opportunity to help create books that allow "ordinary" folks to share their extraordinary stories.

And to the many hundreds of people who so graciously send in their stories, knowing only some of them will make it into the books. And to my husband, family, and friends for indulging me and supporting me in my profession and my passion, storytelling. And to you, kind readers, for celebrating the magic of Christmas, and these magical Christmas stories, with us.

Contents

 Introduction

I will honour Christmas in my heart, and try to keep it all the year.
~ Charles Dickens, *A Christmas Carol*

I believe in the Spirit of Christmas.

I believe, because no matter how old I get or how curmudgeony I might be feeling, when the holiday season rolls around, I *feel* the Christmas Spirit in the air and in my heart. It is palpable—unmistakable—and everywhere. . . .

It is in the wide-eyed wonder of children whispering their deepest desires to a jolly old elf with a long white beard, a funny hat, and a red fluffy suit, who will cross the entire world on a giant sleigh pulled by flying reindeer and make their wishes come true.

It is in all of "Santa's helpers" who keep that

magic and the hope it inspires alive.

It is in those who have little but give what they can and in those who have plenty and give generously, so that others won't do without.

It is in the heartfelt greetings of "Merry Christmas" and "Happy Holidays," to loved ones and strangers alike.

It is in the merrymaking and communion, the brilliant decorations and dazzling lights, the fragrant trees and wreaths, the culinary treats and feasts—all to celebrate the season of caring and sharing, and the birth of Christ, who taught the true meaning of compassion and charity.

It is in voices lifted in verse and song, singing praise to the Shepherd of Love and to His message of peace and joy to the world.

It is in all those holiday cards and letters that, regardless of the words written on them, say, "I think about you. I care about you. I wish you well."

It is in family get-togethers and festive gatherings in which the gifts of love and laughter, friendship and family, and time spent together, actually being together, are more cherished than any fancy gifts money can buy.

It is also in each "perfect" gift carefully selected or handcrafted and lovingly given to fill a need or a void, or to fill a heart with gladness.

The Spirit of Christmas is in every shared joy and in every act of kindness during this wondrous time of year. Yet, in the hustle and bustle of the Christmas season (which seems to begin earlier each year) and with the commercialization of this sacred holiday (which seems to get more brazen each year), it is easy to lose one's Christmas Spirit. I know I have on occasion—almost. Fortunately, I'm blessed with family and friends who are incontrovertible Christmas enthusiasts and who always remind me of its true meaning.

One Christmas evening about thirty years ago, my middle child, Christine, climbed onto my lap for a mommy snuggle. Usually boisterous (*hyper* was the word most people used to describe her), Christie was unusually quiet and reflective that day, only partly because she and her older sister had giggled and whispered and tiptoed repeatedly to their upstairs bedroom window hoping to catch a glimpse of Santa until the wee hours of the night, and then had awakened at dawn to rip open and play with their new toys, and then to play and eat and argue and chase and play some more with their cousins and aunts and uncles, and oh my, to open even more gifts from uncles and aunts and grandmas and grandpas and godparents and babysitters and friends. Phew! I get tired just thinking about it.

As Christy and I cuddled in the rocking chair, rocking and gazing at the tree, she sighed deeply and said, "Know what, Mommy?" (This was during the year that she prefaced every sentence with "know what?")

"What, Christie?"

"I love Christmas."

"So do I, sweetie."

"I wish we could have Christmas all the time. Every single-dingle day." ("Single-dingle" was another Christie-ism, one I suspect she picked up from her great-grandpa Frank, who loved Christmas, too.)

"If we had Christmas every day, it wouldn't be as special," I said. "Besides, you little greedy goat, what would you do with all those presents?"

"Not *presents!*" she said, looking up at me, her brow furrowed with tiredness and sincerity. "*Happiness*. That's why. So we'll have bunches of happiness every day."

Needless to say, I couldn't promise nor provide the happiness of a four-year-old's Christmas every day of Christie's life. But I have made an effort to keep the Spirit of Christmas alive all year, trying to shine the light of happiness whenever and on whomever I can.

Yes, Christie, there is happiness in Christmas—bunches and bunches of happiness. And goodness. And comfort. And love, most of all.

These gifts of the Christmas Spirit—joy, compassion, peace, hope, love—can be found within the heartwarming stories you are about to read in *A Cup of Comfort for Christmas*. May these blessings grace you every day of the year, every year of your life.

—*Colleen Sell*

A Christmas to Remember

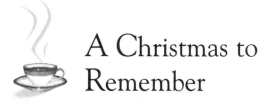

He toddled around the corner and into the living room, where he stopped cold. His little mouth dropped open, and the light in Ryan's eyes rivaled the glow of the lights on the Christmas tree. What he saw there were two big shiny Tonka toys, a tractor and a fire truck with a ladder. There were other packages, too, mostly from his grandparents and one or two small ones from me. But those would have to wait. He only had eyes for those trucks.

I looked at Mike, who was looking at Ryan. I couldn't tell whose eyes were brighter.

"Those are for you, Ry," I said.

That was all the encouragement he needed. He ran to the fire truck, climbed on, and rode three laps around the living room on top of the truck. Then he hopped off and lay down on his belly, pushing the tractor and making engine noises.

He's such a boy, I thought. Looking at Mike, I could visualize him doing the same thing when he was a kid.

Before long, Ryan had both Tonkas upside down, examining every inch. Ryan wanted to know every detail of every toy he had. If the Tonkas hadn't been welded, he would've surely taken them apart to have a better look. He was Mike's son all right. In fact, in only a few minutes, Mike was right down there with him.

At two and a half, Ryan was the perfect age for Tonka trucks. At thirty-three, Mike was the perfect age to enjoy them with his son. I'm not sure which of the two of them had the most fun.

Eventually, we had to remind Ryan that he had other presents to open. With each one, he seemed happy and excited. What he really wanted, though, was just to play trucks.

But there was something unusual about those Tonkas that Ryan didn't notice. Tonka is famous for using standard colors on its toys, mostly school bus yellow. Ryan's tractor was navy blue, and his fire truck was wine-colored with a silver ladder. These weren't the Tonkas you buy in the store now. They were the good old hard metal ones no longer produced. For weeks, Mike had sat in his lonely little trailer in the evenings, cleaning, repairing, and sanding those trucks to make them good as new. Then he had painted them. Now he was getting the payoff for his labor of love. Ryan was in kid heaven.

It had been a hard year for Mike, Ryan, and me. Only a few months earlier, I'd asked Mike to move out of our home permanently. We still cared for each other, but his alcoholism and all the bad things that came with it had finally succeeded in beating the life out of our marriage, and I'd given up trying. After the initial bitterness, we became friendly again. Though our marriage was definitely over, because of Ryan, there would always be tender bonds between us.

The breakup left both of us financially drained. I felt dismal after Thanksgiving, when I realized that Christmas was coming soon and I had no money. I could manage to get a small tree and maybe after that, if I really squeezed, I could come up with five dollars to buy Ryan a few Hot Wheels. That was it. But compared to Mike, I was practically rolling in the dough. Of course, he would spend Christmas Day with us and share our tree. But I knew that he would be hard-pressed to have even one extra dollar to buy Ryan anything at all.

It was depressing at best. I wanted so much to make a wonderful Christmas for Ryan. Not that he needed the toys, and not that gifts are the heart of

Christmas. Ryan would be surrounded by love and celebration and the recognition of the true meaning of Christmas with or without presents. But I'd waited a long time to have a child. And I was anxious to experience the joy that parents feel when they put things under the tree that they know will delight their children.

One afternoon in early December I was on my way home when I heard a man on the radio say that he had a yard full of old Tonka trucks that he was selling for two to three dollars each. They needed some TLC, but they were sturdy and fixable. Ryan had played with Tonkas at a friend's house and adored them. It was the perfect gift for him, and I knew the perfect guy to do the fixing up.

I was so excited, I didn't even stop to call Mike and ask what he thought. He was still at work, anyway. I went straight to the address the man on the radio had given. It was just as he'd said: he had dozens of trucks, but they all needed lots of attention. I scoured the yard looking for the best of the bunch. Some of them had rubber parts that were broken, and I wasn't sure how those could be fixed. Finally, I found two that were well worn but still had all their parts intact. I paid the guy four dollars and fifty cents, almost my total allotment for Christmas. He loaded the metal trucks into the trunk of my car, and I drove to the auto body and paint shop where Mike worked.

Just as he was getting ready to leave, I pulled up next to his car and told him my idea: We could give Ryan a joint present. I bought the trucks, and he could fix them up like new. I was sure Mike had sandpaper and tools, though I wasn't sure about paint. When I opened the trunk and showed him the trucks, he caught my enthusiasm—partly because he would have a great gift for Ryan, one that took Mike back to his own childhood and boyish delights, and partly because he would have a cool project to fill his lonely evenings. I expected him to be interested. But he was more than that. He was thrilled.

As we stood there with the trunk open, Mike's boss came out to see what the excitement was about. Mel had become a family friend, and he loved Ryan. He was about sixty, but I guess guys of any age still love toy trucks, because he had to pick them up and examine them right along with Mike.

"What a great idea," he said, turning the tractor around in his hands. "Real metal . . . how about that! Tell ya what, Mike. Feel free to use any tools or sandpaper in the shop. You can even take some home this weekend. And when you're ready to paint, you can use whatever we have left over from spray jobs. Ryan's gonna love these."

He was right. Ryan loved them at age two and a half, and he loves them now, at eighteen. He still has those two Tonkas. When he was old enough to understand, I explained to him how his dad had spent hours upon hours turning old trucks into new ones, just for him. Ryan no longer plays with his trucks, and his dad is gone. But he can pick them up at any time, look them over, and run his hands over their smooth surfaces. Someday, he might pass them on to his own children. For now, they serve as solid-metal proof that he was the target of a whole lot of love.

—*Teresa Ambord*

 That's Love

With their sixtieth wedding anniversary approaching, my parents still make moon eyes at each other. They've been together since high school, and their love is so obvious it sometimes embarrasses their grandchildren.

Mom massages my father's feet as they watch television. She reads aloud to him on car trips, trims his ear hairs, and fluffs up his pillow every night. She goes on cruises because he loves the sea; she just makes sure she has a bestseller in her luggage.

Because he likes to go grocery shopping, she lets him. She knows he'll bring home at least ten additional items and three of them will always be a can of Dinty Moore beef stew, a bag of dried kidney beans, and a half gallon of some bizarre ice cream, pineapple-blueberry once. She even had a bowl, but just one. He ate the rest himself.

Humming "On the Sunny Side of the Street," she pulls him to his feet and says, "Bill, dance with me," and he does. The dog barks and jumps on them as they waltz past, and Dad twirls her in his arms.

My father, smiling beatifically, sits for hours in Nordstrom's shoe department while Mom tries on staid pumps and shiny black sling-backs. He smiles as he puts four pairs of new shoes into the trunk of their Taurus.

Once, with white hair shining like cake icing, Mom came from her bedroom dressed in a polka-dot jumpsuit, cinched by a wide belt with an ornate silver buckle. My father told her she looked "like a hot mama." She smiled, very pleased with herself.

My father keeps the pantry stocked with her favorites: Hershey bars, Reese's peanut butter cups, and chocolate-covered graham crackers. He stirs up another batch of rich chocolate sauce for her daily ice cream sundae. He doesn't make fun of her when she puts flashlight batteries in upside down. He warms up the car for her in winter, grills steaks just the way she likes them, fixes homemade biscuits on Sunday mornings, and never misses a chance to tell her she's beautiful.

But he's never gotten the hang of buying her a Christmas present. His habit is to slip away at 9:00 P.M. on Christmas Eve and go to Walgreen's. Coming home by 10:00 P.M. with rustling plastic bags, he stays up late waging war with wrapping paper, cellophane tape, and ribbon. Year after year, the same two presents appear under the Christmas tree for my mother: a Whitman Sampler and a large bottle of Prince Matchabelli perfume. Mom always acts surprised as she unwraps them. Then she makes a special trip across the room to plant a kiss on his cheek.

Shortly after Thanksgiving, fifty years into their marriage, Dad hinted that he'd bought a special Christmas gift for his wife. I stared at him. My father doing Christmas shopping in November was unheard of. And he was so obviously pleased with himself.

On Christmas morning, I rooted under the tree branches and found a huge package that looked like a coat box. I turned the tag over and read, "For my beloved wife," in my dad's scratchy handwriting. I shook it. No rattle. Definitely not a Whitman Sampler or a bottle of perfume in disguise.

I handed it to Mom. She looked at me with raised eyebrows. I shrugged, and we both looked at my father. He was about to pop.

"Open it. Open it," he urged, flapping his hands.

As Mom picked at the edges with her fingernail, careful not to tear the paper, my father squirmed.

"Hurry up, hurry up," he said, bouncing in his chair.

"But dear, it's a big piece of paper. I can reuse it."

"I'll buy you all the wrapping paper you want and more. Just open it," he begged.

Finally, she slipped off the Santa Claus paper, folded it in quarters, set it aside, and began to deal with the tape at one end of the box. My father couldn't contain himself. He leaped out of his chair and slit the tape with a rough movement that nearly ripped the top off the box. Then he thought better of his actions, handed it back to her, and sat down, chanting, "Come on, come on."

Mom pulled back the tissue paper and lifted out a pink quilted bathrobe with a chain of daisies appliquéd around the collar and across the top of the single pocket. She smiled and crooned, "Oh, Bill, dear."

But she absolutely refused to meet my eyes.

I looked in my lap and bit my cheeks, trying to keep from laughing.

My father said, "The moment I saw that bathrobe, Mary, I knew it was made for you. I looked at it and thought, *That bathrobe looks just like my Mary.* I didn't even check the price. I just found a salesclerk who looked about your height and weight and asked her to pick the right size. And I bought it."

I marveled even more at my mother's restraint in never telling him the bathrobe that "looked just like her" was identical to the one she'd been wearing every morning for the past five years.

She gave the old robe to Goodwill and wore the new one for another five years.

Now, that's love.

—*Peggy Vincent*

Joey and the Christmas Tree Lot

In my childhood neighborhood, each December a Christmas tree lot would appear. Like magic, an ordinary place, a dry lawn on the corner, would become a forest that smelled like the high mountains.

Within hours of the arrival of the first truckload of firs and spruces, all the kids on our block knew about the tree lot, and a dozen of us would converge on the site. The two young men in charge were friendly, goodhearted guys trying to make an honest buck. They slept in a tent at the side of the house and ate at the Thrifty drugstore soda fountain, across Vermont Avenue.

My family lived in a ramshackle Victorian house that needed paint, near the University of Southern California in Los Angeles. Ours was a busy city neighborhood. Dogs barked, drivers honked, kids yelled, streetcars rumbled, planes hummed overhead, blue jays screeched, and doves cooed. At night we heard neighbors fighting, yowling cats, crickets, and distant sirens.

Living there, we got to know grad students, black and Latino families, Asians who ran small neighborhood businesses, and the Strelnikovs, whose two blond daughters wrote in Russian. On Thirty-First Street, two homes took in elderly widows who rocked on the front porch and always had time for kids. They belonged to us, part of our special world, a unique block unlike any other. We had deaf Mr. Parker who ran the apartments next door. Penny, in one of the apartments, was working on her doctorate in psychology. She had a lover and everyone whispered about it. Mrs. Clark, the hard-bitten chain-smoker who lived above Penny, cooked at an all-night café downtown. We had the Richmonds, who had eight kids and ate steak on payday. And we had Joey.

Joey showed up one fall, shortly before the Christmas tree lot opened. The kids knew about him the day the family moved in. Gail Rinn spotted him on the lawn, sitting alone, a small, dark-haired boy with no arms and a big smile. Because his legs were not right, he could not walk, but shuffled along on his bottom, looking at things in the grass and flowerbeds. Joey said hello to everyone who walked past.

I rode my bike over to take a look. I didn't know what to say. So I said, "Hi."

Joey's bright, big-eyed smile told me he was happy to see me. We talked.

He said, "Even if you are twelve and I'm nine, we read the same books, so we can be friends." He looked me in the eye and charmed me. "I saw you doing bike tricks in the street. You're as good as riders in the circus. You could make your own circus, you know."

What good ideas from such a little kid.

I said, "Our cat can do some tricks. He could be in it. And my sister can hang upside down on a trapeze in the tree."

"If you do the circus, I want to come and watch you practice."

Joey's dark-haired mother came out and sat in a chair on the porch. Her husband was a grad student, she told me. They would stay several years.

I straddled my fat-tire bike, with the big rusted basket mounted over the front wheel. "What happened to Joey?"

Joey and his mother were totally open about his condition. But it would be much later before I would understand what had caused the terrible deformities while Joey was still a developing fetus.

Gail Rinn came across the street and joined us. She invited Joey to her birthday party, the next week. At the party we found out some amazing things about Joey. All the guests sat in a circle on the carpet to eat, watching with awe as Joey took up his fork between his toes and neatly cut and ate his cake, bite by bite, without a crumb on the carpet. We discovered he could also draw and write and play board games with his feet. Within days, Joey was fully accepted by all of the neighborhood kids.

So, the day the Christmas trees showed up, I rode my bike up the block hoping to find Joey and be the first with the news.

"I already know," he said. "It sounds wonderful."

"I wanted to tell you first." I wanted to do good things for Joey. He was a presence, a powerful spirit.

He said, "Maybe I can get my mother to take me and have a look."

I said, "You know how one Christmas tree smells. Imagine hundreds of them. It's like in the mountains." I drew in a quick breath, smelling the afternoon air, and rolled the bike forward and back as I stood on the sidewalk.

His eyes widened as he looked at me. "What's it really, really like?"

"The Christmas trees?"

"No, riding your bike." Of course, he could not know. "Tell me what it's like."

If I could just explain well enough, maybe he could imagine it. "It's great to pedal hard and get going fast. Sometimes it's really hard to go up a hill, and it's sort of scary when a car passes too close or when you ride off the curb and clunk down. But it's super fun."

"I sure wish I knew how it feels." He sighed and looked around as if searching for a way.

For the first time, I put myself into the body and heart of a person with a disability. He would never ride a bike. Here was this great kid with his brightness and good heart, and he would never get to do something I totally loved, a simple thing like riding a bike.

He scooted across the grass to get closer to me and examined my machine. The empty sleeves of his shirt lifted in the light wind. "It looks big enough, that thing you carry things in. I wish you could put me in that basket, and take me for a ride. But I know you never could."

His face was delicate, his smooth cheeks pink with health. I blinked. Then I perceived the dare and could not ignore it. "I could do it, you know. I know how. But it would be way too dangerous."

"I don't care." He stared at the bike as his eyes brightened with hope. "I don't care. I want to do it more than anything."

"But what if I crash?"

"You won't. I know you won't. I saw you doing circus tricks with Gail, and I saw you riding with your sister on the back. You won't crash."

"Your mother will get mad at me." Had I already decided I could do it?

"It's not your idea. It's mine. I'll tell her I made you do it. I won't let you get in trouble. Believe me. We have to do this."

My heart beat faster. It was a big risk, far bigger than swinging off the garage roof on the rope tied to the avocado tree.

I leaned on the bike, looking into his bright eyes, weighing the options. The last time I'd crashed was when we had practiced standing on our bike seats, doing ballet arabesques. The question was, *Could I be serious enough, pay close enough attention, to be totally sure Joey would be safe?*

"Please," Joey asked, small on the grass. "I really, really want you to. I want you to do it so much. You have to do this for me. Nobody else would ever do it, only you." He hesitated. "Nothing will happen. Come on."

I climbed off, set the kickstand so the bike stood firm on the sidewalk, and walked over to Joey. He didn't look very heavy.

"Oh, yes," he said. "Just pick me up and put me in there."

I lifted him awkwardly, as his clothes slipped around. He was heavier than I'd thought. Bracing the front wheel of my bike between my knees, I placed him carefully in the basket. "Is that okay?"

He scrunched around a bit, his legs crossed in front of him. "Okay. This is fine. Where shall we go first?"

Holding tight to the handlebars, I moved around to the seat, kicked up the stand, and pushed off slowly.

Joey at once began to hoot with glee. "Wow, oh boy. Wow, the wind." He started giving orders. "Don't go too fast. Don't go in the street. Be careful. Go faster. You can go even faster now."

His weight in front made steering tricky. We rolled down the sidewalk, past homes and lawns and parked cars. We dipped for a driveway, and Joey gasped. Staunch and responsible, I focused on riding smoothly, holding the front wheel straight, no jerking, no sudden movements. Another driveway dip, Joey hooted, laughed, and squealed. I laughed. Then he howled, a long plaintive wolf call of triumph, "*Owweeeeeee!*"

"You aren't even scared," I said.

"This is so great." He panted with excitement. "This is great. Let's go clear to the corner."

It was just a bike ride; that's all it was. But Joey had the wind in his face, the world rushing past, all that risk and all for the first time.

Usually bossy with younger kids, I was happy to do whatever Joey wanted. This was just for him. I said, "Want to go see the Christmas trees?"

"Yes. Let's go. But be very careful. Not too fast. Oh, boy. I can see the Christmas trees. Slow down."

We approached the dense lines of small evergreens, rigid on their wooden X-stands. I snapped off a green sprig and held it to Joey's nose. I said, "I love this smell."

"Let's go in," Joey said. "Let's go right in between the trees. Like in a real forest."

The tree guys were busy with customers. I pushed the bike into the secret hidden space between two rows. The soft branches brushed my arms and Joey's face. He bent forward to protect his eyes, giggling and squealing. A sharp forest smell broke from the needles as we rolled down the narrow lane.

"I love this," Joey said. "This is the greatest thing."

When we returned to his house, Joey's mother ran out, frantic and furious. "I can't believe you took him. It was absolute idiocy." Her voice was as shrill as a madwoman's. She snatched her son into her arms, still shouting. "This is my boy, my boy."

I wanted to tell her that we had done something wonderful. I wanted to explain. His mother held him tight, yelling over his head about how stupid I was.

Joey shouted over and over, "It was all my idea." He tried to make her listen. But she was too upset. The two of them shouted at each other until she carried him inside and left me standing alone in their yard.

In her fear, Joey's mom could envision only what might have been lost and could not imagine the joy her son had been given. But I knew and Joey knew. And we would always know the amazing power of our glorious adventure to the Christmas tree lot.

—*Barbara Hazen Shaw*

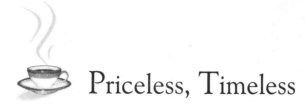# Priceless, Timeless

Dad anchored the wooden stand to our ceiling-high Christmas tree as it lay on the living-room floor, while his five children, ornaments in hand, cheered him on.

"That should do it," he said, jostling the stand to make sure it didn't wiggle.

Grabbing the center of the trunk, he pulled and shoved until the enormous tree stood upright in the far corner of the room. Whistling "Deck the Halls," he strung the lights. Then, hoisting his hefty frame onto a chair, he topped the tree with a fluffy-haired angel whose lopsided halo made me smile.

"We need a new angel," my brother Clifford said. "Her wings look like a glider ready to take off."

"Shh," I whispered. With wartime shortages in 1944, I knew that one didn't replace angels, or much else for that matter, on a whim.

Most of our neighbors selected trees from Anderson's Christmas tree lot, but Dad had borrowed Mr. Tatton's truck, hiked up the cold, snowy mountainside, and cut our tree himself—his Christmas gift to his children.

Soon we were busy hanging handmade ornaments, making popcorn chains, and smoothing out each tinfoil icicle before carefully placing it on the huge tree. The tree glimmered and glistened.

My sixteen-month-old brother, Stan, pointed to his reflection in a shiny red ornament. "Baby," he said, giggling and pressing his nose against the glowing ball.

Dad chuckled, bent down, and kissed Stan's cheek. I could almost feel Dad's soft mustache against my own skin. I smiled and sat on the sofa, awaiting Dad's annual reading of the Christmas story, a Christmas Eve tradition in our home.

I was nine and a half. For weeks and weeks my brothers, Charley, eleven, and Clifford, seven, and I had been saving every penny we could earn and find. The three of us had raked leaves, shoveled snow, delivered newspapers, and babysat. We had gone over to the fairground after the carnival left town to look for change that might have been dropped. Dad didn't know it, but we kids had a plan and even our mother was in on it.

"What would you like for Christmas?" Dad asked when he saw us leafing through our Sears Roebuck Christmas "Wish Book."

Mama smiled and winked. I winked back.

"I'd like a doctor kit," Charley and Clifford answered.

"Me, too!" I said.

Dad's eyebrows curled up over his glasses, and his hazel eyes looked at each of us in turn. "You got those last year," he said. "Wouldn't you like something different?"

My brothers and I exchanged knowing looks and shook our heads. We knew that, in addition to the doctor kits, a fat Christmas stocking crammed with candy and nuts, a tart red apple in the toe, and a juicy orange plugging the heel would await each of us on Christmas morning. We also knew that the sibling who had drawn our name would surprise us with a yo-yo, a box of watercolors, or a treasured book from the library rummage sale. Besides, with our doctor kits, we could give each other pretend shots, listen to heartbeats with the plastic stethoscopes, and ration those miniature multicolored candy pills so they would last until Easter. Most important, we knew that our parents could afford what we'd chosen.

Mama taught fifth grade; Dad was the principal of her school and two others. Being eighteen years older than my mother, who was more relaxed, Dad was from what he liked to call "the old school." Translated, that meant he periodically administered standardized tests to all the students in his three schools to monitor their scholastic progress, and he personally checked each response with an answer key, red pencil in hand. Each test contained several sections, all of them timed. Dad did a lot of clock watching.

Correcting the tests he didn't mind, but administering them rankled his soul. A few weeks earlier when he'd come to administer the tests in my classroom, I'd watched as he'd waited until the second hand of the clock on the wall was straight up and then uttered those frightening words, "You may begin!" and then later, "Stop!" That's when I got the Christmas idea.

"I must send the order tomorrow," Mama told us ten days before Christmas, "to make sure it gets here on time."

Every evening before we went to bed, Charley, Clifford, and I counted the money we had saved. We needed three more dollars.

"Let's sell homemade Christmas candy," I suggested.

"What about vinegar taffy?" Clifford said. "We can color one batch red and the other batch green."

Mama nodded. "Good idea. I'll help you."

Charley measured the sugar, water, butter, and vinegar and set it on the stove to boil. The kitchen smelled worse than when Mama poured the vinegar rinse over my head after she washed my hair. When the mixture boiled down, Mama dropped a little into some cold water.

"It's done!" she said. "See the firm ball?"

She poured the candy into pie tins to cool and added the food coloring. We buttered our hands and pulled, stretched, and twisted until the taffy changed texture. Quickly, we laid the taffy ropes onto waxed paper covered with powdered sugar. Grabbing her long kitchen scissors, Mama cut the taffy into bite-sized pieces.

"Bundle up," she said as we prepared to go door-to-door, peddling our ribbon candy throughout the neighborhood. "It's cold out there."

"You take this side of the street, Charley," I said. "Clifford and I will take the other side."

For an hour we trudged through the snow, knocking on doors, usually hearing "No, thank you," and occasionally selling a few pieces of taffy. My hands felt like icicles. So did my toes.

"This candy is probably frozen solid," Charley said. "I know I am."

Clifford blew on his hands. "I am, too. Can we go home?"

I gave him one of my looks. "Let's try the next block."

As we climbed the steep hill, the wind whistled

through our coats and rattled icy tree branches in the tall oaks. At the top of the hill, music poured from Dr. Whiting's house on the corner. A blazing fire shone through the picture window, and people filled the living room.

"Let's skip this house," Charley said. "They're having a Christmas party."

It was too late; Mrs. Whiting must have spotted us. The door opened wide, and a tall woman with a kind face smiled at three half-frozen children.

"Would you li-ike to buy s-some Chris-s-st-mas taffy?" Clifford asked, his teeth chattering.

"I believe I would," she said. Without asking the price, she took the remaining candy and, after a few words with her husband, slipped three dollars into Clifford's coat pocket.

Sliding down that hill toward home, our feet scarcely touched the ground.

Now, it was Christmas Eve. Wood crackled in the fireplace, and a warm glow filled the room. The rest of the family had joined me on the sofa, where we sat gazing at our newly decorated tree with the slightly bedraggled angel at its crown.

"It's time for the Christmas story," Dad announced.

He opened the family Bible and began to read the familiar story of the birth of the Christ child, while Mama, her brown eyes shining, cradled her own little son in her arms.

When the story ended, we gathered around our ancient upright piano. Charley played the piano, and we sang all three verses of my favorite carol, "Silent Night." I thought about Mary, Joseph, and the baby Jesus. I thought, too, about the shepherds in the fields and the wise men who had journeyed from afar, bringing gifts to share with the holy child. As I sang, the spirit of Christmas surrounded me, filling my heart, touching my soul.

Later, as I lay in my bed upstairs, I thought about another gift . . . the special one.

"It's wrapped and hidden in the tree," Mama whispered, tucking my covers around me and kissing my cheek. "I'll tell the boys."

When Christmas morning dawned, we lined up from youngest to oldest in the hallway downstairs. We couldn't go into the living room, not until Dad had peeked into that room, turned on the tree lights, and announced in his booming voice, "Old St. Nick has been here!"

We waited happily, but didn't have to wait long. Eyes aglow, we scampered into the living room. Under the tree, gaily wrapped gifts awaited us, and our stockings were right where they always were on Christmas Day, hanging like colorful rag dolls over the back of the sofa, filled to the brim with candy and nuts.

We each took our stocking and settled down on a spot on the floor to collect the surprises that awaited us. Mother handed Dad the presents one at a time—"To Mary, from Santa," or "To Charley, from Kaye," he read—until all the gifts had found a home.

Only one child opened his gifts at a time, beginning with the youngest. The rest of us savored that person's joy and excitement. I helped my little brother Stan.

Dad, being the oldest, always opened his presents last. This Christmas brought him the usual array of grown-up necessities: a pair of socks, a large eraser for his schoolwork, three red pencils, and a small collapsible leather coin purse. He received each gift with an expansive grin and a heartfelt, "Thank you."

"Well," Dad announced, when nothing but discarded wrapping paper adorned the worn carpet, "we've had a wonderful Christmas!"

"Wait a minute," Mama said. "I think I see another gift."

Reaching back into the branches of the sweet-smelling pine tree, she drew out a small package wrapped in gold and tied with tinsel. "To Dad," she announced, handing the gift to him.

Dad slowly unwrapped the box and looked inside. A long sigh finally broke the stillness. Tears spilled down my father's cheeks as he held his eighteen-dollar stopwatch by its golden chain so that we could all admire his treasure. Then he opened the case and in a quivering voice read the inscription: "To Dad, with our love."

Time has tucked away many years since then, and many Christmases have come and gone, but the Christmas of Dad's special gift will always be my favorite.

—*Mary Chandler*

This story was first published in GRIT magazine, December 12, 2000, under the title "Dad's Special Gift."

Simply Magic

I t's dark. The black sky sparkles with the brilliant light of distant stars. It's cold. And the laughter and chatter of excited anticipation make puffs of smoke with every joyful breath. Everyone is happy: Mom, Dad, and all five kids—ages eleven months to seven years. We've just come from Christmas Eve Mass and look forward to a delicious dinner.

Okay, it's really McDonald's. But the drive-through isn't too crowded and the servers actually get our order right. We sit down to our meal. Carols play softly. The Christmas tree glows. Fries by candlelight. The evening flies.

It's nearly bedtime.

"Mom, the cookies!" Our daughter's voice conveys an urgency suggesting Santa's imminent starvation should we fail to supply cookies.

I open the Tupperware, and she carefully arranges

cookies on a decorative paper plate. Her fastidious attention to the plate's palette of color, shape, and flavor create a delicious opportunity for the baby. While our culinary artist considers how an additional chocolate chip or sugar sprinkle cookie will affect the composition of Santa's snack, our sly baby makes his move. His tiny, chubby fingers cling to the table's edge. Stealthily, he pulls himself up. In the twitch of a reindeer nose, the baby grabs a cookie, drops to his bottom, and crawls away with cheetah-like speed.

"Mom!" shrieks our little girl.

I scoop up the baby as he gums his sugary catch. "Don't worry. I'll put him to bed."

I take him and his two-year-old brother up the stairs. Neither really protests; they're tired after a busy day of play. As our daughter finishes her cookie masterpiece, our middle son, who has trouble with certain consonants, studies it critically.

"What if Hanta gets hursty?" he asks.

Our oldest considers the problem and then searches for pencil and paper. He touches the eraser to his lips, leans toward the paper, and with purposeful determination begins: *Dear Santa*, he prints carefully, forming each letter to his second-grade teacher's exact specifications.

"What are you writing?" his ever-curious sister asks.

"Shh! I have to concentrate." He continues: *The*

milk is in the— Panic strikes. "Dad, Dad. How do you spell 'fridge'?"

My husband pauses as he sweeps French fries. "*R-e—*"

"How can 'fridge' start with an *r*?" our phonetically aware daughter interrupts. "*Fridge. F-r-ig. F-r-ig.* I think it's an *f.*"

"Well, it's really called a refrigerator," my husband says as he sweeps up a fry mixed mysteriously with pine needles.

"Re-frig-er-a-tor. Re-frigerator," repeats our little girl.

Our son's pencil hits the table with impatience. "How do you spell it?"

"*R-,*" says our girl, "*e-*"

"No!" protests our insulted second-grader. "Dad!"

"I was only trying to help," pouts our wounded first-grader.

My husband begins, "*R-e—*got that?"

"*F-r-i-d*"—he dumps the dustpan of fries—"*-g-e-r-a-t-o-r.*"

"Got it." Our writer thinks, then adds, *Thank you for coming.*

Everyone present signs the note after the word *Love.* My husband forges the babies' names.

I come down the steps and announce bedtime. They're willing tonight, even eager, but first they want to check Santa's progress one last time. We log onto the Internet and go to NORAD, the North American Aerospace Defense Command. From its North Canadian post, this government organization tracks Santa's sleigh and reindeer as they depart the North Pole and travel around the world. We reach the site and an up-to-the-minute report begins. An official voice announces that right now Santa is leaving Rio de Janeiro. We watch the video showing his sleigh flying gracefully around the Christ the Redeemer monument and heading toward the United States. NORAD projects that Santa's arrival time in our hometown will be around midnight.

"He's coming! He's coming!" they cheer.

"Come on. It's time for bed," I say.

There's no argument tonight. They all run up the stairs. I follow slowly to make sure they brush their teeth and say their prayers. They know they must go to sleep. Santa won't come until they're asleep. But it's hard to sleep. It's impossible to sleep. It's all too wonderful. Tomorrow is Christmas. Tomorrow! A glance out the window. Then a long stare. The flashing red light on the radio tower—it's . . . Could it be? I want to believe it, too. But if it is Rudolf, they must go to sleep. Now. Santa's coming.

A mad dash of little sock feet and quick leaps into bed. Covers pulled warmly about them and a moment of silence. Suddenly, quiet.

Then a little voice asks, "Do you hear Santa yet?"

"*Shh.*"

"I think I hear him!"

"*Shh!*"

Giggles and laughter and quiet whispers and whispers that get louder, and then "*Shh.*" Again and again. But finally the "*shh*" lasts. It's quiet, and it stays quiet.

Sleep. And then a sound. It's late or early, the middle of the night. I'm awakened and I make the mom rounds, checking on the kids. The babies are sleeping soundly, curled up in their cribs, their little bottoms skyward. My next little guy is oddly arranged with most of his body avoiding the soft mattress, seeking the hard plastic of his racecar bed. I pull the blanket around my daughter on the bottom bunk, and as I look toward the top one, my oldest pops his head up.

"Did you hear that, Mom?"

"You have to go to sleep."

"I think it was Santa."

"Go to sleep. I love you."

"Can we check, Mom?"

"Check?"

His sparkling eyes and innocent belief win my heart. What's a few more lost moments of sleep? In just one or maybe two more years, a rooftop noise on Christmas Eve might make him merely roll over. For the moment, whatever woke us holds the promise of childhood magic.

"Okay, but we won't go down. We'll only peek from the steps."

He springs from his bed, not a bit tired.

"*Shh*," I say.

"Oh, okay." And he begins an exaggerated tiptoe out the door and into the hall.

I take his hand as we creep down the steps. My own heart pounds with excitement. One, two, three . . . from about the sixth step we can see. Just a night light burns. The tree is not lit. The room is mostly dark, but somehow the shadows shine. I watch my little boy, his eyes wide, his smile broad. He glows with awe and happiness.

"All those presents. . . . Look! Look at the stockings. . . . Mommy! Mom, he ate the cookies. He ate the cookies."

"*Shh*." But I'm even happier.

We hug with happiness. We sit on the steps and linger in this wonderful night. But it's very late, or very early, and we must get some sleep.

My little boy hurries to bed. I fix his blanket and kiss his cheek. He falls asleep immediately. I lie awake. My dreams are visions of joy. Tomorrow is Christmas, but there will be no better present than tonight.

—*Barbara L. David*

Grandma and Grandpa and Karen

Although I talked to him on the phone and wrote him letters, it had been more than five years since I'd seen my grandfather. Our last meeting had been at my grandmother's funeral. When my husband, Frank, and I finally found the time and money to fly to Illinois to spend Christmas with him, I was flooded with excited anticipation.

I envisioned walking through the door of the same cozy house I remembered from my childhood visits, the one Grandpa had built himself as a young man. There would be homemade desserts beckoning from the countertops. Crunchy, undisturbed snow would blanket the front yard, just begging to be used in a snowball fight. Grandpa had even promised to buy a real Christmas tree.

I could picture every detail perfectly, except for one thing: Grandpa's new girlfriend.

I'd never met or spoken to her before, but I'd heard the news from family: Her name was Karen, and she was twenty-five years younger than my eighty-year-old grandfather—younger than my father, even. She was living with Grandpa, at least part of the time. I'd found out she'd known him for many years. In fact, before her husband had died, Karen and her husband used to spend time with my grandparents. Despite their age differences, the two couples had clicked. I would be meeting a stranger, but Karen would not; she "knew" me from years of friendship with Grandma and Grandpa.

Despite all the things that might make a grand-daughter wary, I had already decided there was no reason not to like her. My grandfather had been married to my grandmother for more than fifty years before she died of cancer, and her death had been devastating to him. Grandpa deserved to be happy again, and from what I'd heard, Karen was making that happen.

When Frank and I arrived in Illinois three days before Christmas, Grandpa and Karen were waiting for us at the airport. Karen, who had fluffy blond hair and glasses, gave me a warm hug. As the four of us stood at the baggage claim area and spoke, it was immediately evident how content Karen and my grandfather were together.

Grandpa's house was just as I remembered it. In fact, it was a little spooky. My grandmother's presence was everywhere—in her pictures on the shelves, in her homemade afghan on the couch, in her handwriting on the ancient Tupperware. After spending decades in that house with my grandfather, there was no question that her memory belonged there, but it was that very fact that made it strange for me to watch Karen move comfortably among her things.

Warm-hearted and gracious, Karen did everything right. She cooked for us, cleaned, made us feel welcome, and made Grandpa smile. I genuinely liked her. Still, I couldn't help wondering how Grandma would have felt knowing her old friend had slid seamlessly into the life she had once owned. Would it have been a comfort, or a betrayal?

The question bothered me, and I thought about it on and off as I watched Karen and Grandpa together. They snuggled beside each other on the couch, their legs covered with Grandma's afghan. I thought about my own history and the times I'd felt betrayed. If Grandma could have chosen Grandpa's future girlfriend, would she have wanted her to be a stranger, someone completely separate from the bond Grandma and Grandpa had shared, or would she have wanted him to choose a friend of hers, someone who knew everything—maybe too much—about the past?

The ability of another woman to remember and discuss Grandma could be a gift or a curse;

undoubtedly, it is an element of power. Of course, I knew the question of what Grandma would want was hypothetical; Grandma was gone, and it was Grandpa who would decide what happened next. Karen was a good woman and she made him happy, and for that I was grateful. End of story.

On Christmas morning, I heard whispering. Halfway through our present-opening celebration, Karen muttered, "I can't wait anymore!" Abruptly, there she was, standing in front of me, looking excited, eager, and nervous. She handed me a large package and told me to open it next.

The label confused me; the present was from "Grandma and Grandpa and Karen." What did that mean? My first fleeting thought was that Karen had called herself "Grandma" and then thought better of it, but that didn't make sense. Everyone watched as I opened the gift.

As I unfolded what turned out to be a huge, colorful quilt, Karen said, "Your grandma saved the material from the dresses and outfits she sewed for you when you were little."

The quilt was amazing. Framed against a white-and-purple background were bright, cheerful squares of material representing outfits from my childhood, beginning with my birth year of 1972 and continuing through 1980. Embroidery in my grandmother's handwriting explained each square.

"Rompers, 1 year old, 1973" was a red, blue, and black plaid peppered with fuzzy white Scottie dogs. The fabric that read "Christmas 1976, blouse, age 4½" was a jumbled mass of flowers, triangles, and staircase shapes in yellow, orange, green, tan, brown, black, and white—very 1970s. One square, also from 1976, was more familiar than all the rest. It was white satin speckled with tiny turquoise dots and tiny tulips. At the top of each tulip's delicate green stem was a raised blossom of sky blue fluff. The four-year-old me had loved the blouse made of that fabric. She probably never would have believed that she'd one day give up such cheerful clothes for dark, solid colors that didn't draw attention.

Karen spoke again. "She had finished all the embroidery and picked out the pattern. I just put it together." She looked at my grandfather. "Your grandpa chose the border."

Around the quilt's edge, Garfield smiled his sly grin while Odie let his tongue drool on the quilt squares. Garfield had been my favorite cartoon as a girl.

Grandpa said, "Your grandma started that before she got sick, but she never got to finish it. I was just going to throw that stuff away, but Karen offered to finish it for you."

I ran my hands over the fabrics on the quilt—silky, cottony, fuzzy, and textured—then looked up at Karen's hopeful smile.

I immediately stood and hugged her, holding her tight and thanking her for the quilt. I felt many things—grateful, happy, honored—but most of all, I was shocked. What shocked me was not the quilt itself or the story of how it had come to be, but the realization that my questions had been answered. Suddenly, I thought I knew how my grandmother would have felt about Karen.

There were two very different ways to interpret Karen's gesture, but my heart knew the right answer. This was not a woman trying to show up my grandmother or take her place. Despite the fact that she now had my grandmother's husband, had my grandmother's home, and had even finished my grandmother's quilt, Karen's moving among Grandma's things showed not domination of them, but respect.

She respected my grandmother enough to let her presence remain, respected her enough not to mind when Grandpa talked about Grandma, respected her enough to know what half a century of marriage signifies. Karen had made this quilt not to outdo my grandmother, but to honor her. Her completion of the quilt that Grandma hadn't had the strength to complete was as much a gift to my grandmother as it was a gift for me.

I think Grandma would approve.

—Alaina Smith

The Porch People

The winter was not going well for our young and growing family. I was expecting our sixth child, and my husband had been out of a steady job for nearly two years. Taking whatever temporary work he could find, we were able to make our monthly obligations, but with Christmas coming in a few days, we were saddened that we would be unable to provide our children with gifts.

One evening, the doorbell rang and we opened it to find a big box on the porch—and no one in sight. We dragged the heavy box inside and discovered that it was stuffed full of food and candy. The children danced around excitedly as we pulled out everyday basics like macaroni and cheese, as well as the makings for a delicious turkey dinner with all the trimmings, including apple pie filling and a pre-made piecrust.

The next evening as we helped the older children with schoolwork and bathed and readied our younger ones for bed, the doorbell rang again. This time we found a smaller box, but were just as thrilled by its contents: a small ceramic Nativity set. Again, whoever had delivered the box had disappeared by the time we'd opened the door.

We let the children choose a place of honor for our new gift. After they decided who should stand by Joseph and that the lamb needed to be next to the shepherds, my husband and I spent a few reflective moments with our children on the meaning of the upcoming holiday. We reminded them that Mary and Joseph had been desperately poor, having not even enough money to provide a room in which Mary could give birth to her baby son. I asked the children how they would feel if they knew that their pregnant mommy would have to go out in a barn to have our new baby there. They looked very solemn. I gently told them that Mary and Joseph did not have any money to give gifts but that didn't mean they didn't love their baby.

Our four-year-old reminded us that we didn't need any money, for surely Santa Claus would bring us presents. We went to bed that night in agony, wondering how we would explain to our children on Christmas morning why they had received no gifts.

The next few evenings our children anxiously

awaited the return of the "porch people." Their only disappointment was that they were unable to catch them in the act, for every night, another box filled with Christmas goodies and decorations appeared on our front porch.

Two days before Christmas I opened the back door to shake the rugs and found another box. This one was filled with wrapped gifts bearing cheerful tags addressed to our children, by name. There were several gifts for each child and even a few for my husband and me. I hid the presents so the children wouldn't find them and looked forward to sharing the secret with my husband. After a discouraging day of job hunting, I knew he would appreciate some good news.

When my husband came home later that day, I beamed as I told him of the box I had found on the back porch. Wanting him to have a small surprise on Christmas morning, I didn't mention that there was also a package for him. He gave me a weary smile and headed for the shower.

That night, I had a hard time keeping my children away from the windows. They spent a good deal of time peeking outside hoping to catch a glimpse of the porch people. They even offered to take out the trash. Finally, I got the Monopoly game out of the closet and soon had the older ones interested in buying property and avoiding the "Go to Jail" square.

Whenever they heard an unexplained sound, all the kids would look up expectantly and ask, "Is it the porch people?" I couldn't ruin the surprise of Christmas morning by telling them that we'd already received an extra-special box earlier that day, so I tried to distract them with games and stories.

I also wanted my children to learn something valuable from the porch people. So, I asked them why they thought the porch people would do so many nice things for us. Were they family members? People from our church? Neighbors? Whoever they were, we decided that they must love us.

My nine-year-old then gave an analogy that brought tears to my eyes. "The porch people are like the Wise Men, who brought gifts to baby Jesus just because they loved Him."

Several months later, my husband found a permanent job, and I gave birth to a healthy son. Soon, Christmas was upon us again. Our financial situation had improved and we were able to provide a lovely holiday for our family, but the porch people had taught us an invaluable lesson. That Christmas, we became porch people to another family in need, because, like the Wise Men, we love Him and all His children.

—Kenya Transtrum

Silver Belles

My best friend, Olivia, and I had spent an entire Saturday afternoon at the mall, searching for a dress for me to wear to my husband's office Christmas party. My goal was to find a dress that would make me look thin. Olivia's was to max out her credit card. Every outfit Olivia tried on rewarded her postdivorce weight loss. Every dress I struggled to zip up made me look as round as the snowman-shaped sugar cookies I'd baked, and eaten, last week.

By midafternoon, the bottoms of my feet ached and Olivia was suffering nicotine withdrawal. I bought a robe for my husband, Ed; gloves for my mother-in-law; and a new spatula.

While I scanned the crowded corridor for a dress shop we might have missed, Olivia supplied a minute-by-minute report of the vacation to Sedona, Arizona, that she and her boyfriend had taken.

"Then one brilliant afternoon, Harrison and I hiked to a mountaintop," Olivia said in a dreamy voice. "Can you believe it? Me, a person who gets dizzy looking out my second-floor apartment window."

Since her divorce, Olivia had done all sorts of remarkable things. She'd gone hiking and deep-sea fishing, streaked her hair bright blond, and become a Pilates instructor at a local health club.

As we dodged a baby carriage and then an elderly woman in a wheelchair, Olivia said, "Harrison and I were holding hands on top of the mountain. We were surrounded by red rocks and green trees and the brightest, biggest blue sky I'd ever seen. All of a sudden, a white feather landed on my arm. Just like that. Harrison said it was a sign."

"Of what?" I asked.

Olivia shrugged. "I can't remember now. He's always finding meaning in the ordinary. What I do remember is how he started kissing my neck and, well, you know how it is."

"Of course," I said, trying to imagine Ed and me cuddling on a mountaintop. I tried to recall whether we'd said anything meaningful to each other lately, but all I could remember was discussing with him whether we should refinance our house. I could see us on the couch in front of the television, but not overlooking a vista. We needed to get out more.

Olivia and I passed a window display of skinny

mannequins clothed in tight black dresses and aluminum trees festooned with red and green ornaments.

"Oooh, look at the silver trees," I said.

"So sixties," Olivia said. "I need a cigarette."

I touched my friend's arm. "When I was a little girl my family had an aluminum tree. My mother was allergic to real trees. I'd get so excited when my father pulled the big box we stored it in out of the closet. We had this funky electric color wheel that would spin and change the tree's color. I'd stare at the tree for hours trying to decide which color I liked best."

"Really?" Olivia asked, removing a pack of cigarettes from her bag. "Which color did you like best?"

"I never could choose just one," I said. "During the day, when the sun shone on the tree, it sparkled as if the branches were sprinkled with diamonds."

Olivia fidgeted. "Let's go find a place where I can smoke."

"It'll only take a minute to look in here. Maybe the aluminum trees are a sign this is where my perfect holiday dress is. You know, like your feather," I said.

Olivia looked longingly at the pack of cigarettes. "Okay, but remember, I get cranky without nicotine." She sighed. "I am supposed to quit. Harrison hates when I smoke. He says I'm soiling my lungs."

Fifteen minutes later we were in adjoining dressing rooms trying on clothes. While inhaling into a pink dress, I called to Olivia, "If I hear 'Joy to the

World' one more time, I'm going to start a picket line against Christmas carols."

"Susanna, sweetie, relax. You're just exhibiting typical signs of a woman desperate to find the perfect dress. Release and let it come to you," advised Olivia.

The Sedona vacation and yoga teacher boyfriend had given Olivia a New Age attitude toward life. In the years before, when she was still married, she would have complained right along with me about the holiday crowds, rude salesclerks, and pricey clothing. Lately, she was so wrapped up in her own blissful world, I felt like she didn't hear anything I had to say.

"Easy for you to say, Miss Serenity," I said. "You're a size seven. I'm hoping not to burst the seams of this size twelve."

"Susanna, do you think it's totally indulgent of me to buy myself another negligee?" she asked.

"What's wrong with indulging?" I said, thinking I'd been doing plenty of it myself lately, but not with lingerie. All my vows to lose fifteen pounds had been forgotten after Labor Day. I'd munched chocolate at Halloween, eaten stuffing at Thanksgiving, and baked batches of sugar cookies every weekend. I had only myself to blame for a serious case of tummy bulge.

I glared at myself in the dressing-room mirror. The pink taffeta dress that had looked so sweet on the hanger had turned mean.

Olivia called, "How does it look?"

"The words 'circus tent' come to mind. I should know better than to risk pastels. Black is the only safe color," I grumbled. "The lighting is horrible in here. My skin looks like I have hepatitis. There's no way I had this much flab under my arms when I left home."

"Stop being so critical," Olivia said. "Let me see."

"I'll spare you," I said, struggling to free my hips from the dress's vicelike grip. "I thought for sure those aluminum trees in the window were a sign that my perfect dress was here."

Outside the dressing room I found Olivia admiring a sheer purple negligee trimmed with white feathers. "I've already spent too much money, but I've got to buy this. I love looking sexy for Harrison."

I thought of the faded Phoenix Suns T-shirt I slept in and said, "Let's go eat lunch. I've had enough of fun house mirrors and dresses made for preteens."

As we wove our way around groups of giggling teenage girls, young couples holding hands, and tired-looking women with children, I half-listened to Olivia's plans to spend Christmas skiing with Harrison in Colorado. Lately, I'd begun to wonder whether Olivia and I were growing apart. We'd been friends since college; gotten pregnant the same year; supported one another through teething, potty training, and our kids' first day of school. We had cried together when they went off to college.

As the years went by, it became impossible to ignore the tension, cruel comments, and nasty tones of voice that had developed between Olivia and her husband, Dan. I spent countless hours on the phone listening to Olivia pour her heart out about her failing marriage. The day Dan moved out, she came over and sobbed. Then we drank red wine and danced barefoot to a Cher compact disc.

I felt mean and small for not being happier for my dear friend's newfound happiness. It's just that there were times when I felt as if she was racing ahead of me, trying all sorts of new things, meeting new people, and leaving me behind. I had the same husband, same job as a freelance writer for a local newspaper, same lumpy thighs and flabby tummy. She seemed to be the pretty, slim, and single rabbit to my plodding, old, married turtle.

We decided to splurge and, instead of eating at the food court, go to a pretty restaurant in the mall where we could be served our pasta salads and white wine by a good-looking waiter.

With "Silent Night" playing softly in the background, Olivia speared a cherry tomato and asked what I thought of plastic surgery. "You know, to freshen me up a bit. I was thinking of having my brows lifted. Get rid of these handbags above my eyes."

I crunched into a carrot and said, "Ed claims he loves me whatever I look like. Then a thin model with long blond hair comes on the television, and he gets this glazed look. I expect at any moment he'll drool."

Olivia nodded. "Dan drooled over golf. But, honey, you know Ed still loves you."

I gave her arm a little squeeze. "Thanks for reminding me. It's just that I wish I could get that spark for life that you seem to have these days. I'm in a slump."

Olivia, looking over my head and motioning the waiter to bring us our check, didn't disagree.

I left the mall that day without a dress, even though the office party was less than a week away. Over the next several days, I kept busy writing a story about illegal immigration, which gave me a good excuse not to go shopping. Frankly, I didn't want to face myself in another dressing-room mirror. I decided to wear a black wool dress I'd worn several years before to a funeral.

The day of the Christmas party, I returned home from grocery shopping to find a large cardboard box at my front door. After putting away the milk and chicken, I opened the box and pulled out a silver, knee-length dress. It was soft and slinky and looked like thousands of tiny mirrors sewed together. It glittered like the sun on new-fallen snow. The dress not only fit perfectly, it also slimmed my waist and flattered my bustline, and the slit up the side made me feel sexy. I stood in front of the mirror and twirled.

The enclosed gift card read:

This is just the thing to light that spark.
Merry Christmas, my beautiful friend.
Love, your very bestest friend for life,
Olivia

That night I put on diamond stud earrings and a pair of silver high heels I was lucky to find in my daughter's closet. I applied some of the red lipstick I'd bought on the spur of the moment a few months earlier but had been too shy to wear. I used aqua eyeliner to bring out the blue in my eyes.

Trying to appear more confident than I felt, I strolled into the living room, where Ed waited for me, watching the evening news.

"*Ta da!*" I said, spreading my arms and smiling.

"Wow!" Ed said and turned off the television.

"It's not too much?" I asked.

He grinned. "It's just right."

As I danced the night away in my husband's arms, I couldn't help but think of Olivia. She'd given me a Christmas present even better than the sparkly silver dress: the reassurance that our friendship would pass the test of time, no matter how much our figures and the world around us changed.

—Susanna Anderjaska

Silent Night

The first day of the Christmas shopping season found me standing in the checkout line of a discount store, waiting to purchase swim fins and goggles. A large display of wrapping paper and sparkling Christmas decorations stood near the checkout, as twisting, stuffed Santas rocked around the clock. It was not even September.

The days passed. My favorite restaurant sported paper place mats challenging my knowledge of Santa's reindeer. Fake trees started popping up in stores, first in out-of-the-way corners, sneaked in as guilty contraband, then moved to the aisles adjacent to the jiggling cartoon Santas. I still wore white sandals.

Grocery stores offered Christmas giveaways. Charities took applications from those in need and solicited donations to fulfill those holiday wishes. One of my children practiced her viola for the

Christmas concert. The other asked for a photograph so he could make a Christmas gift for me at school. The Salvation Army bell ringers caught me as I exited the stores, while Halloween candy cluttered the clearance tables.

It was finally cool enough at night to wear a sweater. Homecoming games were in full bloom. My son played a turkey in the school pageant, and three of his tail feathers fell out. My daughter doggedly sawed her way through "We Three Kings" each night in preparation for the concert. Everyone kept asking, "Have you finished your shopping yet?" It was almost Thanksgiving.

Years ago, I holiday shopped year-round, bought and wrapped my presents by October, and decorated everything but the dog in red and green. I baked until I collapsed in a cloud of flour. But the official Christmas season kicked off the day after Thanksgiving.

Then the holiday season began to grow bigger and to start sooner, leaking into the early part of November. And then Christmas stock started sharing shelves with Halloween costumes, and then with back-to-school supplies. And then came that day in August when I had to skirt Christmas displays to find the snorkeling equipment. I decided I'd had it.

"I'm tired of Christmas. I wish the whole thing would just go away and leave me alone," I told my husband.

But it didn't; it just grew worse. My children created wish lists big enough to support the budgets of
Third World nations. The baking and shopping had
become just dreaded chores. I refused to play anymore.

And then I took my dissatisfaction to the next
level: I ran away from home.

A few days before Christmas, we packed up the
minivan and drove to the mountains of North Carolina, where I'd rented a cabin. The air was clear and
fresh and hung heavy with the threat of snow. But
still, even surrounded by breathtaking beauty,
Christmas just didn't seem right. The magic was gone.

We spent a couple of days sightseeing. One afternoon as we settled back in front of the cabin's fireplace,
my son's stomach rebelled and he threw up all over his
bed. *Great,* I thought, *Now I've got to find a place to wash
clothes . . . two days before Christmas, no less.* Though I'd
tried to escape the holiday frenzy, it seemed to be in
some back room of my mind, yelling, "Ready or not,
here it comes!" I most certainly was not.

Washing clothes seemed to suit my black mood.
I put the soiled linen in the back of the van, and we
drove to a little town a few miles over the mountain,
where I remembered passing a Laundromat.

There were several people inside the once-white
building, which was now a dingy gray, its large picture windows yellowed from cigarette smoke. A pair
of migrant workers was folding clothes at one end,

while a young couple with a little boy put coins into the machines. I loaded two washers and plopped down in one of the hard plastic chairs to wait. My pouting kids decided to sit in the car; my husband walked around outside.

The door opened and a middle-aged woman and a girl of about sixteen walked in. They'd pulled up in a wreck of a car, an old station wagon covered with more rust than paint, and lugged in a large plastic basket overflowing with dirty clothes. The two filled washing machines until they'd emptied the basket.

The woman, who I assumed was the girl's mother, sat in a chair near the dryers, her back to me. Even from behind she looked weary, her graying hair pulled off her face into a bedraggled ponytail. She wore a sweater with more holes than yarn and hugged it close to her. The girl, all lean angles with a tangle of dirty blond hair, stood by the woman's side. She gently rubbed her mother's shoulder and smoothed her hair.

Then the girl started humming, so softly I could barely hear her over the chugging washing machines and humming dryers. After a moment, the humming changed to singing.

In a soft voice, she worked her way through the opening bars of "Silent Night." Her long, thin fingers continually stroking her mother's hair, she closed her eyes and her voice gradually swelled and rose to fill the room. In a pure, sweet alto, she sang the last stanza of the classic carol.

"Sleep in heavenly peace."

The song was as familiar as my own childhood, when my grandfather would stand next to me on Christmas Eve, sharing the big hymn book as we joined in song. Outside, cars whizzed by on the narrow strip of asphalt curving through the mountain town. As the last weak rays of the sun streaked the sky, the older woman leaned into her daughter's side, while the closing notes washed over us, warm and familiar.

"Sleep in heavenly peace."

The door opened, throwing an icy blast into the room. It was my son. I shook off the moment and pulled clean linens from the dryer and folded them. My husband stepped back inside to help. As we walked outside, I felt something cold and wet hit my face.

"It's snowing!" my son said.

"So it is," I said. "What do you say we go home?"

"You mean back to the cabin?" my husband asked.

"No," I said. "Home. Our home."

He smiled. "Let's go get our things."

I climbed into the van. As we pulled out, I saw the two women bathed in the dim glow of the fluorescent lights, digging into their pockets for quarters, laughing, sharing some private joke. I leaned back in the seat and watched the fat, lazy snowflakes dance in the headlights. I thought about the girl and the gift of song she'd given her mother and how, by providence, she'd also given it to me, a stranger. And I remembered the child who once stood at her grandfather's side, singing "Silent Night" in a high thin voice, playing counterpoint to his rich tenor. And how at the end of the hymn, both his favorite and mine, he reached down and took my hand, folding it into his bigger one and radiating his love: for his God and for me.

Yes, I thought, *it really is time to go home.*

—Carole Moore

Oh! Christmas Tree

It was the first Christmas without both of my grandparents. They had lived full, rich lives into their eighties, leaving behind five children, four grandchildren, and five great-granddaughters. Grandpa had died first, after a brief bout with bone cancer, at home on Thanksgiving night. Several years later, congestive heart failure finally won the battle and took Grandma in her sleep one January night. It was best that Grandpa had died before his wife of more than fifty years. I don't know how he would have gotten along without her—not that his absence hadn't been hard for her, but she'd managed.

The tradition in my Slovak family is to open gifts on Christmas Eve after enjoying a home-cooked dinner of sour soup (which only those of Slavic heritage can appreciate) and fish. With grandmother no longer there to prepare the old-fashioned Christmas

Eve meal, we debated for weeks whether to continue the tradition. But we decided it just wouldn't be Christmas Eve without our Slavic fish and sour soup.

My mother and her younger sister got out their mother's handwritten recipes and gave it their best shot. After all, they had assisted her with the preparations for years. How hard could it be? My mother baked the traditional nut and poppy seed rolls, which were even tastier than Grandma's. And she found just the right kind of fish for the entrée and mushrooms for the soup. The rest of us did what we could: peeled and boiled potatoes, cleaned and prepared the vegetables, set the table. We even remembered my grandmother's sugared, stewed prunes.

Sixteen of us shared the new, old-fashioned Christmas Eve dinner, which turned out to be almost as good as Grandma's. Everyone was glad that we had decided not to give up at least that tradition.

After doing the dishes and opening the Christmas presents, the adults sat around the living room, reminiscing as families do on holidays, while the children went off to play together. My first cousin from Wisconsin and I had shared every Christmas Eve of our childhoods together and now we had daughters close to the same age. It was fun to watch our children get to know each other. The freshly cut tree was beautifully decorated, as always, with lights and ornaments that had been around forever.

It stood in a corner of the living room where my grandparents' favorite chairs had always been, as if to fill the void of their absence.

As I sat across the room, gazing at the tree, the oddest thing happened. The tree shook. Gently, as if someone had reached in, grabbed it by the trunk, and given it a single shake. All heads turned at the melodious sound of the ornaments tinkling gently, sweetly, momentarily hypnotized until the ornaments settled back into place. No one spoke. Then we all spoke at once.

"What happened?"

"Who did that?"

"Where are the kids?"

One uncle grabbed his camera and took a picture of the tree.

We did our best to explain what happened, but couldn't. It was December in Illinois; no windows were open, no door had opened or closed to cause a breeze. No one was even walking around; everyone in the room was sitting. We looked under the tree for a toddler; all the kids were in another room on the other side of the house. We jumped on the floor. The tree didn't move. (The house has a concrete floor. Nothing moved.) Needless to say, there was only one topic of conversation the rest of the evening.

A few weeks later, my uncle brought his pictures around. On the photo he'd taken of the shaking tree was a pair of round, hazy, but obvious gray spots. Lens glare? Maybe. Spirits of Christmas past? We will never know. Film is sensitive; there could be a technical explanation. Then again, maybe not.

We still discuss this event at family gatherings, especially at Christmas, when we all sit around looking at the tree and hoping, I think, that it will move again. But it never has. And we've never found a physical explanation for the tree's shaking. What we do know for sure is that we all had the same feeling when it happened: that Grandma and Grandpa had found a way to tell us they were together again and happy that we had carried on our family Christmas tradition.

—Mauverneen Blevins

What Stocking for Mother?

"Glenn?" It was my mother on the phone. *Why was she calling me at college in the middle of the week?* "You need to come home."

My heart sank. I didn't want to hear what she had to say next.

"There was a thunderstorm. . . ." A sob stopped the flow of words.

"Hi, Glenn?" A man's voice. "This is Pastor Richards. Your mom wanted to tell you herself, but she can't right now. Glenn, it's your father. He was on the commuter plane that flew into high-voltage wires. There were no survivors."

My father had worked with politicians and community groups from all over the state. Hundreds of people came to the funeral. But before week's end, relatives had gone home, friends had returned to their lives, and Thanksgiving loomed ahead—with just my mother, my sister, Lori, and me.

I was glad to go back to college. Though I felt guilty, I was relieved to escape the muffled cries coming from my mother's room, weeping into a pillow.

Three weeks later, I returned home for Christmas break. Grief hung heavy on my mom. Lori and I wished we could ease her burden.

In our family, tradition called for us children to hang stockings on the fireplace. My parents never had stockings for themselves. But earlier in the week, Mother had said she was going to skip the stockings that year. Lori was fourteen, and I was twenty. It wasn't like our belief in Santa Claus was going to be crushed, and it was one less duty for her.

After supper on Christmas Eve, Mother went to her room. Lori and I stared at the television.

Lori turned to me and said, "Why don't we go ahead and fill the stockings? At least there would be something more to do in the morning."

"Yeah, you're right."

We picked through the pile of gifts under the tree and found some small ones to put in our stockings. Then we took some candies out of the little Rudolph bowl and dropped them in.

"Hey," I said, "How about we make a stocking for Mom, too?"

Lori looked surprised. "A stocking for Mom? Mom and Dad don't . . . I mean, they never . . . well

. . . Sure. That would be a good idea!"

We looked at the two stockings hanging on the mantel. Glitter spelled "Lori" on one; embroidered stitching spelled "Glenn" on the other.

"Should we use one of these for Mom?" I asked.

Lori thought about it. "She has socks."

I looked at my feet, then at the stockings, and back at Lori. "That would be awfully small."

"How about pantyhose?"

"Perfect!" We looked at each other and smiled.

Later, when Mom went to brush her teeth, Lori snuck into her room and grabbed a pair of pantyhose. We tacked them to the mantel, putting the tacks right through the nylon.

Our parents had always put an orange in the bottom of our stocking. So, I got an orange from the refrigerator, and Lori plopped it into the pantyhose.

We both jumped as the orange thumped on the floor. We stifled giggles behind our hands. One leg stretched to four feet with a round lump in the toe while the other leg hung tiny and wrinkled.

"What about that one?" I asked.

Lori got another orange and put it in. *Thump!* We had to laugh at the elongated pantyhose with bulbous feet tethered to our fireplace.

We scooped up the small gifts for Mom from under the tree and put them in the "stocking." They disappeared into the extraordinarily large legs, leaving hardly a trace.

"What now?" Lori asked.

I took some knickknacks off the end tables. "Here, wrap these."

Knickknacks, a hairbrush, a toothbrush, a kitchen towel, all were called into stocking-stuffer duty. The pantyhose drooped further and still had plenty of space left.

We poured in the rest of the bag of the Christmas candy.

"We need more," Lori said.

"What about the dish of candy in the family room?"

"I'll get it."

In went the candy . . . and the dish, both wrapped first, of course. Still, the stocking wasn't full. We raided the pantry, adding a package of opened cookies (taped closed) and a can of cherries. Bulging at all angles, the sagging pantyhose begged for more.

"This is not going to hold."

"I'll get some nails."

"The hammer's in the basement."

A bottle of hand cream, bars of soap, a letter opener. For an hour, we wrapped items from all over the house.

We stood back to admire our work. "Egads! Those look like Godzilla's mother used them!"

We had to cover our mouths to keep our laughter

from waking Mom.

The next morning, the first Christmas in twenty-six years without her beloved by her side, Mom was reluctant. She delayed coming out of her room.

Lori and I waited in the living room. When we looked at the monstrosity bulging over the fireplace, we giggled. But we also worried that Mom might be too sad to take a joke.

Finally, she came in and sat down—walking right past the fireplace. She gave us one of the watery smiles we had seen too many of lately. Then she glanced over at the fireplace.

She did a double take and looked confused. We couldn't help grinning.

She walked over to the light tan nylon covering nearly the entire fireplace. She looked inside the lumpy legs of the pantyhose, stretched to twice their normal size and holding half our household goods. And she began to chuckle. We laughed our way through opening all those gifts—each of which had to first be wiggled and jiggled out of four feet of stretchy, clingy material. Lori and I missed our dad and Mom missed her husband that Christmas, but our love for each other had, um, stretched to cover the occasion.

—Andria Anderson, as told by her husband, Glenn

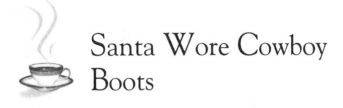

Santa Wore Cowboy Boots

When my son, Erik, was nine years old, he taught me a lesson I will never forget.

That year, my husband, Walt's, job transferred from my hometown of St. Louis, Missouri, to Fort Huachuca, Arizona. At first, leaving the Midwest for another part of the United States seemed like an adventure. I felt enchanted with the stately mountains, the vast desert, and the wide, Arizona sky.

Our children Julie and Erik loved being able to ride their bikes year-round and having a yard they didn't need to mow. Decorative rocks and cacti landscaped our "Southwestern" front yard. Mostly dry dirt covered the back, except for a sprinkling of mesquite trees, which were about the size of holly bushes back home.

On weekends, we explored our new surroundings. We hiked the Coronado Mountains and visited the historic towns of Tucson, Tombstone, and Bisbee. On one outing we ventured across the border to Nogales, Mexico, where we bought gifts from street vendors. In Nogales, a trio of raven-haired teenaged girls dashed up to Erik and rubbed the top of his light blond head.

When I asked, "Why are you doing that?" one girl yelled, "For good luck!" over her shoulder as she ran giggling down the street.

That small gesture made me realize how different our new home was from Missouri, where children with blond hair and blue eyes were as common as dogwoods in springtime.

By autumn, Walt was traveling a lot with his job. The kids busied themselves with schoolwork and their new friends, while I dealt with dust storms, scorpions, and snakes. Every day, the weather forecast sounded like a broken record: sunny and mild, sunny and mild, sunny and mild. Back home, the redbuds, sweet gums, and maples—"real trees"— would be crowned in their glorious fall colors. Even more than I missed the changing seasons, I missed my parents, my brothers and sisters, and the friends I'd left behind.

As the days grew shorter, I began to feel lonely, isolated, and depressed. I longed for the smell of fresh-cut grass, the sight of a lightning storm rolling across the evening sky, and the sound of rain cascading down the roof. One afternoon while Walt was at work and the kids were in school, I retrieved an umbrella from the bottom of a closet, dusted it off, and opened it up in the bathroom shower. Standing beneath the umbrella, I tried to imagine standing under a soft gray Missouri sky in the pouring rain. It just wasn't the same.

Thanksgiving Day, I hit my lowest point. During a telephone conversation with my family in Missouri, my sister Kathleen reminded me of our traditional day-after-Thanksgiving shopping marathon with our kids and our youngest sister Bridget.

"It won't be the same without you and the kids tomorrow at breakfast with Santa," she said. "If we get snow, it'll cut into our shopping time. Of course, you can shop all day in the great weather you have in Arizona."

That night I didn't even finish dinner and went to bed before the evening news. I couldn't bear to hear another sunny-and-mild weather forecast.

The next morning, I decided to try and make the best of the day. I'd promised to take Erik to visit Santa and to take Julie, who, at twelve, no longer believed in Santa Claus, shopping for Christmas gifts. I thought if we stuck to at least one of our holiday traditions, we might feel more of the Christmas spirit. But instead of things getting better, they got worse.

At the breakfast table, Julie and Erik argued over

whose turn it was to read the cereal box, who was supposed to feed the dog, and who got to ride in the front seat when we went shopping.

"You're both sitting in the back," I said. "And if you don't stop arguing, we'll stay home."

My threat seemed to work; the kids quieted down, but by the time we'd put on our shorts and T-shirts and hopped into the car, I was in a crabby mood again. I turned up the radio as we drove to town so I wouldn't have to listen to the kids bicker over whose fault it was that I was so angry. I just didn't have the energy to turn the car around and spend the day inside.

When we got to the department store, Julie hurried off to the music department, while Erik and I stood in line behind the velvet ropes and the fake snow of the North Pole. At the front of the line, I stared in disbelief at the store's version of Santa. Instead of having jolly red cheeks and a snow-white beard, he had a deeply lined, suntanned face. His beard was scraggly and gray. Silver and turquoise rings adorned his nicotine-stained fingers. I looked down at his feet and shook my head. Instead of shiny, solid-black boots, this Southwestern Santa wore pointed-toe snakeskin cowboy boots. The only thing missing were spurs and a ten-gallon hat.

I sighed and mumbled, "I don't believe it. Can't these people get anything right?"

"What's wrong, Mom?" Erik asked.

"Nothing," I sighed and nudged him forward. "Go on. You're next."

"Well, now, little pardner," Santa said, putting his arm around Erik. "Have you been behaving yourself and listening to your mom and dad?"

Erik glanced at me, and then nodded.

"Is that right, Mom?" Santa asked, looking in my direction.

"Most of the time," I said. "He's usually well behaved."

My son stood taller after hearing the compliment.

"And what is it that you want Santa to bring you, little pardner?"

Erik's face lit up as he recited the list of presents he hoped to see under the Christmas tree. He finished with, "A skateboard and a new bike."

Santa asked, "Anything else?"

Erik stared at his feet. "For my mom not to be so sad all the time."

My face grew as red as Santa's suit and my heart sank when I heard my son's words. Until then, I hadn't realized how much my homesickness had been affecting him.

Peering over his wire-rimmed glasses, Santa said, "How about it, Mom? Can you give our little pardner here a smile every once in a while?"

Blinking back tears, I nodded. Santa handed Erik

two candy canes and said, "Here's one for you and one for your mom."

After we left the toy department to find Julie, I gave Erik a big hug. "I'm so sorry," I said, wiping my eyes.

When Julie saw us she said, "What's wrong, Mom? What did he do now?"

"Nothing," I said. "It's what I've done, but things are going to change, starting today. How would you guys like to go home and make Christmas cookies?"

"Cool!"

We stopped at the grocery store and filled our cart with chocolate chips, nuts, coconut, and other sweet ingredients. On the way home, I rolled down the windows, turned off the radio, and the three of us sang Christmas carols. When a roadrunner darted in front of the car, we all laughed out loud—something we hadn't done in a long time. I realized, as we drove past the mountains and under a canopy of clear, blue sky that although each place has its own special beauty, there's nothing as beautiful as the laughter of a child.

That day, my son taught me that Christmas isn't about snowflakes or evergreen trees or holly bushes or jolly-faced Santas in red suits and black boots. It's about embracing the blessings in your life . . . and sharing them with those you love.

—*Donna Volkenannt*

 # A Joyful Noise

I was not thrilled about playing holiday music at some nursing home. At fifteen years old, there were ten thousand things I would rather be doing on my first day of Christmas break. None of them included dragging my trumpet and music stand to the Wesley Glen Home for the Elderly to entertain. I had committed to do it as part of my required sophomore service project hours, and my mother insisted I go.

Mom dropped me off in the family station wagon, assuring me that she'd run to the drugstore to fill a prescription and return soon, in about thirty minutes. I turned to her with pleading eyes.

"Go," she said. "You'll make people happy."

I rolled my eyes and slid out of the car. As I walked through the thick, revolving doors into the drab building with fluorescent lights and about ten shades of ivory, white, and taupe, I started to panic.

Had Mom left yet? Maybe there was still time to back out. I don't want to do this.

It wasn't really that I wanted to be off sledding with my friends, or at the mall or movies. Nursing homes made me uncomfortable. My only experience with them had been annual visits to see Grandpa Grzegorczyk at the Midland Home for the Elderly. Visits with him usually included brief reintroductions by my mother.

"Dad, you remember Sarah? Sarah is the middle child. And this one is Bridget, she is nine and getting so tall."

My sisters and I would line up to give an unacknowledged kiss on the cheek or to bestow a skittish hug. After the reintroductions and mandatory embrace, my father would whisk us kids off to the House of Flavors to give my mother time alone with her ailing father. That was my full experience with nursing homes and the people who lived in them.

Lost in the momentary flashback, my cheek held briefly against my grandfather's cool, gaunt face, I jumped when a nurse in white scrubs shouted to me.

"Good, you're here!" she called, ducking into a storage bin for something.

"Uh, have you seen a saxophone or a trombone?" I asked timidly. (My fellow band members and I referred to each other by our instruments.) I may not have wanted to be there, but at least I wouldn't be alone. I scanned the foyer for signs of the rest of the brass trio.

But the nurse was doing a million things at once and didn't hear my question. Instead, she rushed past me, arms full of linens. Turning around halfway down the hall, she called out, "Cafeteria's down the hall, to the right!"

I wandered, uncertain, through the corridors. I tried to resist looking in the individual rooms, but most doors were open and I caught glimpses of still bodies and slack-jawed faces. Some of the residents slept, some stared at the television screen, and some gazed out toward the hall. I was catching too many glances by looking into the rooms, so I glued my eyes to the floor and continued the search.

I found the cafeteria, led there by the unsavory aroma of reconstituted mashed potatoes, defrosted turkey slices, and some kind of Veg-All dish. As I turned into the room, a sagging candy cane garland bopped me in the face. An artificial Christmas tree with paper ornaments stood against the backdrop of institutional furniture. Attendants in white emerged from the kitchen, balancing stacks of trays and distributing them to the people quietly waiting at the tables or in wheelchairs.

Where was the rest of my trio? Did I get the time wrong? Had the concert been canceled? I couldn't very well play a brass version of "God Rest Ye Merry

Gentlemen" without the harmony line. I would sound stupid. I'd just have to explain that I couldn't play without the other two musicians.

But before I could excuse myself, a voice rang out, "Ladies and gentleman, we have a special guest today from Bishop Watterson High School. She has come to play the Christmas music for our holiday party!"

I froze. In that moment of confusion, I glanced around and spotted an old upright piano sitting off to the side of the room.

I went to the piano and sat down. The white keys were discolored and some of the black ones were chipped. When I played a few scales, I was surprised to find the instrument was mostly in tune.

But I had no sheet music and hadn't played the piano in ages. I would just have to wing it and rely on musician's memory.

"Joy to the World" came to me first, and then "O Christmas Tree." I played basic versions and had to improvise in places, but it sounded all right.

I had just launched into the second verse of "Silent Night" when I felt a warm presence beside me on the piano bench. A blue-sleeved arm belonging to a very old man rested next to mine. *What does he want?* I wondered. *Does he think I'm someone he knows?* Not knowing what to do, I continued playing until I saw his large, gnarled hands extend toward the keys.

He turned his head and looked into my eyes.

"Um, hello," I stammered. "Do you, uh, play the piano?"

Slowly, he looked down, staring hard at the keys.

I tried again, "I'm not very good. I just play the trumpet now, in the school band."

His silence made me feel even more awkward. The only way to relieve my discomfort was to start playing again. I raised my hands but hesitated when I saw his hands tremble.

Silence.

Then music. Beautiful music.

Grand, sweeping melodies filled the hall. His hands crossed over each other, stretching to reach the lower notes. *Chopin? Grieg? Liszt?* A familiar classical piece, rich with crescendo and pianissimo, alive with passionate glissandos. He barely looked at his hands as they floated over the ivories, up and down the keyboard. I couldn't take my eyes off of them.

The nurses, who a few moments earlier had been rushing around, had stopped all activity. In fact, the whole room was at a standstill. Forks were put down, and even the kitchen workers had stopped to watch and listen.

He went on for almost ten minutes and finally, delicately revealed the ending of the piece. He humbly rested his hands in his lap, looking down. The room was charged, the notes still reverberating in the air.

I whispered, "That was beautiful. They must love having you around here."

A nurse appeared next to us, her face electric. "Oh, John!" She beamed. "We didn't know you could do that!"

I turned to the woman, confused.

"Are you new here?" I asked.

"No, I'm not new." She smiled.

"Oh. Is John new here then?"

The woman leaned closer to me and, our faces nearly touching, said pointedly, "I have been here for fourteen years. John has been here eleven. Never has he so much as touched that piano. We had no idea he could play at all, let alone like that."

Another staff member approached me, her hand on my arm. "What did you do? What did you say to him?"

"Nothing," I said. "I just sat here and played."

"You must have done something!" they both pressed.

"I've got to get Kathy!" one of them said, running toward the reception desk.

Then, John drew my hands together and held them in his. I wasn't afraid; I felt profoundly connected to him. In that moment, I felt the presence of the grandfather I had embraced but never known, and I realized the reason for my being there that day.

Gently, John squeezed my hands and let them go.

He set his wrists above the keys and began to play again. I slid off the bench to give him room. I watched for a while as the whole room lit up with the joy of music. Gathering my things, I reluctantly made my way out to my mom, waiting in the parking lot for me.

"How did it go?" Mom asked.

"Fine," I said, too embarrassed and emotional to tell her what had happened.

But I will never forget how a Christmas chore became a Christmas miracle when two strangers, one in the blush of life and one nearing the end, joined hands and hearts to make a joyful noise that still echoes in my soul.

—*Sarah Thomas Fazeli*

Our Special Box of Love

Our third Christmas together, my husband, Denny, and I lived in an upstairs apartment of a little brick house in Cleveland, Ohio. Our landlady and her husband lived downstairs, and Mr. and Mrs. Webber were lovely, caring people. For Christmas that year they gave us a three-pound box of assorted chocolates, which we were so thankful for. As a young married couple with two babies and another on the way, we had very limited finances and could afford few extras.

The chocolates came in a pretty box, decorated with beautifully drawn holly leaves and berries, and when the chocolates were all gone, I stored our family photos in it for many years. As our family grew, the children all enjoyed looking through our box of pictures, and I always treasured the box, remembering the kind people who had given it to us many years before. After a while our picture supply outgrew our candy box, and we replaced it with a larger one. But I couldn't find it in my heart to throw away the box that had meant so much to me over the years. And I thought it would make a perfect box for a love gift—an extra-special present carefully chosen to delight an extra-special someone in your life, a gift that says, "I know you, and I love you."

That year at Christmas, I decided to put a gift in the love box for my daughter, Cindy. I enclosed a note explaining that she was to handle it with care and that I would expect it back the following Christmas. And back it came—with a special gift in it for me. So began a mom-daughter tradition of buying or making a thoughtful little gift for the one whose turn it is to receive the box the next year.

Year after year, our special love box has held many different gifts: nighties, craft items, blouses, girlie indulgences, all sorts of trinkets, and, of course, chocolate and photos. The most special gifts have been the personal ones that hold sentimental value, such as the year I gave my daughter a handmade antique pillow filled with feathers and covered in black sateen adorned with crewel. It had belonged to her great-grandmother and was made in the late 1800s. Grandma had used it as a neck pillow on the back of her rocking chair. I covered the pillow with lace and added new ribbon ties, and placed it in our special love box. I recently spotted the pillow on my daughter's bed, so I know Cindy cherishes the pillow, even though she never met her great-grandma.

Another gift that brought back lots of memories was a small wreath I made for Cindy and decorated using various simple family heirlooms as ornaments: a thimble, a silver spoon, old-fashioned hair pins used by her great-grandma, and many others items, all belonging either to me, her grandmothers, or her great-grandmothers.

Last Christmas, I received the box. When I opened it, there, to my surprise, was a porcelain picture frame with a photograph of Cindy and me, taken on my sixty-fifth birthday. All around the frame it read, "I Love My Mommy!" That brought tears to my eyes, but they were tears of joy, because Cindy and I have always been close, not only as mother and daughter, but also as best friends.

What started out in 1954 as a very nice but simple Christmas gift from our landlady has become a lifelong tradition between mother and daughter. If Mrs. Webber were here today, I know she'd get a chuckle out of what we have done with the candy box—at its smudges, fingerprints, faded holly and berries, and tape holding it together—and at the cherished, and sometimes comical, expressions of love that it has held over all these years.

And I know that a few weeks before Christmas,

I will get a phone call from Cindy, saying, "Mom, do you have the box this year?" With all the hubbub of putting away our holiday things, we sometimes forget who has the box. This year is my turn with the box, and it is already filled with an assortment of little snowmen, which my daughter collects.

Last year, my husband and I celebrated our fiftieth wedding anniversary, and Cindy and her husband celebrated their thirtieth. We now have eight grandchildren and ten great-grandchildren. Perhaps it is time to fill the Christmas box with family photographs again. Or maybe my granddaughters and great-granddaughters will continue the tradition, swapping love gifts with their mothers, their grandmothers, and their great-grandmothers. Whatever simple treasures we fill it with, I'm sure our special love box will always overflow with memories . . . and love.

—Junella Sell

A Swahili Christmas

"How would you like to go on a photo safari in East Africa for Christmas?"

"A safari in East Africa?" I repeated to my husband.

The idea conjured up images of great adventure—and a pang of reluctance. "It sounds wonderful, but it just wouldn't seem like Christmas, and the boys wouldn't want to leave their friends. . . ."

He handed me a travel brochure, and the colorful pictures of zebras, giraffes, elephants, and wildebeest in Kenya and Tanzania made the prospect more enticing. But we'd have to give up the usual Christmas expenses.

Part of my brain said, *Go, it's the chance of a lifetime!* But another part argued, *It just wouldn't be Christmas without a tree and gifts.*

He showed the brochure to our two young sons.

They looked at the wildlife animals and whooped, "Let's go!"

"No Christmas tree or presents," I warned them.

"Who cares?" they answered.

We made reservations for the two-week trip.

As the departure day approached, I was torn between the excitement of going and the sadness at giving up our traditions. The meteorologist added to my regrets with predictions of a white Christmas. In Africa, it would be summer.

On December 23, we flew to London, and changed planes to fly on to Kenya. We landed, exhausted, at the Nairobi Airport, and were driven by van through the outskirts of town, where natives lived in thatch-roofed huts.

We stayed in a modern Nairobi hotel, whose wall decorations included spears, shields, and bright African wall hangings. The hotel's shops featured carved mahogany busts of Africans, as well as carvings of their animals. We were most definitely in Africa.

We registered, and then headed for the hotel's bank to exchange travelers' checks. At the bank's door, a burly African guard held a baseball bat over his shoulder, apparently to fend off possible bank robbers. It seemed that bank security people were allowed to carry baseball bats, but not guns. An African Christmas would be different indeed.

The next morning, Christmas Eve, we met our

native driver, Adam, outside the hotel. He greeted me with a bright, "Jambo, Mama."

His friendly smile convinced me that he was not calling me a "jumbo mama." Once our luggage was settled, we started out in a zebra-striped minibus.

Riding through the countryside, we bounced on rutted roads for hours before stopping at a colonial hotel, where dusty oleanders bloomed and tea was served on the veranda. Here, Adam picked up our box lunches for later.

Nearby, under the trees, vendors had set up shops for selling drums, handwoven baskets, colorful fabrics, cowhide shields, and Masai calabashes for carrying cow's milk and blood.

"Smell in the calabash," they urged, taking off the lid and holding it out to us.

I quickly backed away from the putrid smell.

They laughed.

We'll buy souvenirs elsewhere, I thought, but the boys thought differently.

"Please, can't we buy one?" they begged. "Please! We'll use our own money."

"Wait till we take them to school!" the boys exclaimed looking over the inexpensive calabashes. "Some kids don't even believe we're going to Africa. They'll believe these!"

We drove on, past scattered villages with more thatched-roof huts. Here and there, Masai men herded their scrawny cattle across the dusty land. The men carried tall spears that doubled as walking sticks, looking as if they had posed for the pictures of Masai in *National Geographic.*

We stopped for cattle and Masai herdsmen crossing the road. My husband opened a side window in the van and pointed the camera toward them.

Adam shouted, "No, no, cannot do!" He stepped on the gas, swerved around the angry Masai, and raced away. "Last week a Masai put his spear through a tourist taking his picture! Masai think pictures take away the spirit."

After some moments, we righted ourselves in our seats and remembered that we were visitors in *their* country. Still, the encounter added to my misgivings.

It was late afternoon when we approached Lake Manyara National Park. My husband read from the brochure: "The lodge overlooks a mahogany forest, marshes, and scrubland, where we find lions lying in the trees and herds of elephants."

But that's tomorrow, I thought. *Tonight we'll spend Christmas Eve in this strange place.*

It was a long day's drive, broken only when we stopped to eat fried chicken from our box lunches and to drink bottled orange juice and water.

We arrived at the rustic lodge in time to wash and change before dinner. Later, in the dining room, a foil Christmas tree stood in the far corner. A few people said,

"Merry Christmas," but the holiday spirit was missing.

After dinner, the lodge manager announced that there would be a program out on the patio. We headed outside for the chairs near a blazing bonfire. Behind the fire stood women wearing bright caftans and colorful turbans high on their heads; the men lined up behind them in white shirts and dark pants.

After we settled down, they hummed a note, and then began to sing in Swahili: "O little town of Bethlehem, how still we see thee lie!" As they sang, their faith radiated like the sparks from the bonfire.

A lump crept to my throat.

Before long, the night filled with "Hark! The Herald Angels Sing" and "It Came Upon a Midnight Clear."

My soul was shaken.

In broken English, the director asked us to sing the last song with them.

My voice quavered as I sang, my English words blending with their Swahili. "Silent night, holy night, all is calm, all is bright, round yon virgin mother and child . . ."

Hot tears streamed down my cheeks. It was Christmas, a real Christmas, not one bound by cultures or traditions.

In Africa, the wondrous story returned to touch me.

—*Elaine L. Schulte*

Toy Soldiers

The rides to Pennsylvania were filled with anticipation. I preferred the train to driving. Something about trains charmed me. I waited anxiously for the train to pull in, eager to see my new baby cousin, representative of siblings I wished to have and didn't.

The downside to the trip was that my mother and grandparents always stayed at a motel and I slept at my aunt and uncle's. Though I hated sleeping away from home, they were loving to me and their apartment was cheerful enough by day, filled with bright sunlight and a balcony overlooking a grassy knoll. But nights in the country were dark and scary, and there was an intangible chill that frightened me. I was a city girl used to city lights. When I visited, which I did nearly every Christmas and on summer vacations and other special occasions, I, of course, had to follow their rules. Also, there was a man in their house—my uncle. I wasn't used to having a man in the house or even other children. I was accustomed to living alone with my mother since her divorce from my father.

Worse, at my aunt's house, I was the oldest child. I was expected to "know better" and to do right. Only I didn't know better and seldom seemed to do right. In my house, I was an only child. I was treasured and pampered by my mother and a loving pair of grandparents. At my aunt's, I was just one of three and the "big girl." So I was embarrassed to tell her how afraid and lonely I was at night.

My aunt was waiting at the train station when we arrived. I was so excited to see my little cousin! But when we walked through the door of their home, my aunt announced that she had found a perfect playmate for me, a boy who had just moved into the apartment next door. A *boy*. That meant trouble. Boys were the ones who teased you at school, pulled your hair, and called you dirty names you didn't understand and your mother wouldn't explain to you. They carried out their threats to punch you in the stomach, so hard you gasped for air. At five and a half, I'd learned that it was best to stay away from boys, and I for sure didn't want one for a friend.

Despite my earnest protests, my aunt went next door and fetched Freddie. He was a little younger than I, having just turned five, but he was much taller. He came in and we were introduced. Neither of us spoke. I knew I was safe as long as the adults were around, but I didn't relish being alone with him. So when he asked me to come over to see his toy soldiers—"Because," he said, looking askance at my doll collection, "there isn't anything good to play with here"—I hesitated.

"Go," my aunt said. "Go. You're a big girl." (There it was again.) "It's only across the hall."

I hated to feel stupid, so I went. And there they were. Two hundred toy soldiers, lined up for battle. Colonels, commanders, lieutenants, officers, privates, and sergeants, ready for action, waiting for Freddie. They all wore green, all two hundred of them. In fact, everything was army green, right down to the tanks and jeeps.

Freddie fell to the floor: "Bang, bang!" he shouted. "Look out, men. The enemy! *Vroom, vroom! Chuggle, chuggle!*" The jeep rode along. "Bang, bang. Duck! Open fire! Charge!"

I was transfixed.

Freddie looked up at me. "Well, what are you waiting for? Come on. Let's play!"

He actually wanted me to play. I dove down but I didn't know what to do. I was used to dressing and holding my baby dolls. I tentatively picked up a soldier and made a feeble attempt at "bang, bang."

"No," Freddie said, looking genuinely appalled. "You just shot one of our men. The enemies are over there!" He pointed.

"They all look the same," I offered.

"Girls," he muttered. "On the other side of this line—over there!" he said, pointing again. "Those are the enemy."

Then he did the oddest thing. He took my hand and placed it in his, over the soldier. "Now say 'bang, bang,'" he said.

"Bang, bang!"

"Great," he said. "Now, try it alone."

We played for hours. It wasn't like playing with dolls, but Freddie made it fun. So much so, that I could hardly wait till morning when Freddie planned to come back for a visit.

The next day I tried out my cousin's bows and magnetic arrows, missing the target every time. Freddie walked over and put his arms around me. "Like this," he said, guiding my hand gently and patiently. I drew my arm back and got a bull's-eye. Freddie's eyes lit up. I remember it as though it were yesterday. "Yes, great!" he said, genuinely happy for me.

Half of me was beginning to trust this male creature, the other half was waiting for him to start teasing or punching me. But it never happened. I had never felt the way I felt when Freddie placed his arms around me. It was a new feeling; a funny feeling. A very soft and close feeling. This, from a boy person. I felt, for the first time in my life, like a girl. A real girl.

Subsequent visits to my aunt and uncle's became less and less gloomy-sounding, and the nights, once scary, were now filled with the anticipation of the next day's bringing Freddie and his ever-ready toy soldiers. Freddie and his platoon seemed to be glued together. If Freddie came over, so, too, did the soldiers. If I went to Freddie's, the men in green stood ready and waiting.

I learned something by playing with Freddie. I learned to put my dolls aside and to play with soldiers, even if it wasn't as much fun. Because Freddie liked it. And he learned, too, I think, that playing father to my dolls wasn't the end of the world. In fact, sometimes I think he almost liked it.

I didn't know firsthand about romance, but I had seen many movies, and Freddie and I began to kiss goodnight, first on the cheek, then once behind closed doors on the lips. I felt pretty for the first time in my life. My family and other adults used to say how pretty I was. But the boys in school made me feel like I had the bubonic plague or something. With Freddie, well, I felt, just maybe, that I wasn't half bad after all.

We visited Pennsylvania again for Christmas. I got the doll I wanted from my mother and a real pearl necklace from my aunt. By now, Freddie and I had known each other about a year and a half. On this visit, we stayed for several days, so I had plenty of time to be with Freddie. When the last day of vacation came, I felt sad. It had been a wonderful holiday and I dreaded going back to school.

My aunt, grandmother, and mother went out shopping. Freddie came over shortly after they left. He was carrying a large, crumpled brown paper bag. Freddie held out both arms and pushed the bag into my hands.

"What's this?" I asked.

"Open it," he said. "Merry Christmas."

I looked in the bag and then up at Freddie. In the bag were Freddie's toy soldiers.

"What?" I said.

"It's for you," he said.

"But they're yours," I said, astonished.

"No, I want you to have them," he said, and he ran out of the door, slamming it behind him, not staying to play.

I just looked at the door, not understanding why Freddie didn't stay to play. Finally, I sat down on the floor and poured out the contents of the bag. Then I counted. Two hundred. All two hundred. Tanks, jeeps, guns, soldiers, everything.

I put each soldier in place, lining them up as Freddie had taught me to do. I organized them into the good guys and the bad guys. I put the kneeling men with their guns on the front line. Then I began. "Bang, bang. *Vroom, vroom. Chuggle, chuggle.*" But it was no use. They just didn't come to life without

Freddie. I sat for the longest time, just staring at the soldiers, missing Freddie.

When my mother returned, she glanced at the soldiers, all neatly lined up on the floor, and asked, "Where's Freddie?" The natural question. "I know he must be nearby." She smiled and pointed, "The soldiers . . ."

After all, Freddie and his soldiers were one.

"He's not here," I said.

She looked at me, puzzled.

"Freddie gave me all his soldiers. He wants me to have them."

My mother gasped. I remember that. She gasped.

"You can't take them," she said. "Freddie loves those soldiers. You have to give them back."

I knew she was right. They were Freddie's. But something in me wanted to hold onto them. My mother must have sensed that in my expression.

"I have an idea," she said. "Give Freddie his soldiers, but you keep one." She waited.

Of course! It was the most brilliant idea I had ever heard. I could keep one!

"Okay!" I said, flooded with relief, as I suspect my mother was also.

"I'll go over and speak to Freddie's mother," she said. I was further relieved that I wasn't alone in this now.

My mother returned after about ten minutes.

"I'm going to tell you something," she said, "but you must promise not to tell Freddie."

I nodded. I loved it when my mother confided in me.

"Freddie has been crying for hours," she said. "He misses his soldiers but he told his mother he wouldn't ask for them back. He wants you to have them."

My heart sunk. I felt so awful that I hurt inside. I had made Freddie, my best friend Freddie, cry.

"You've got to give the soldiers back to Freddie. Tell him you love them and want them more than anything but you want him to have them."

I put the soldiers back into the crumpled brown paper bag, one by one, careful not to damage any of his treasure. I took my mother's hand and the bag, and we went over and rang Freddie's bell. Freddie's mother answered and called for Freddie. He came to the door, his eyes red and puffy from crying. I said nothing.

Then, "Freddie, I can't keep these. I love them more than anything but you love them more and they're yours."

Freddie didn't look happy. Rather, he looked crestfallen. Then I understood.

"But I'd like to keep one. This one," I said as I reached into my pocket and pulled out a soldier. "Meet Sergeant Freddie!"

Freddie's face lit up.

"Can I keep him?" I asked tentatively.

Freddie nodded enthusiastically. "That's a great idea!" he said, reaching out and accepting the brown bag from me. Then he poured out 199 soldiers and began to set them up.

"Can she stay awhile?" He looked up at my mother.

"For just a few minutes," my mother answered, smiling. "We have to catch the six o'clock train."

I dropped down on the floor and began playing, watching Freddie bring the soldiers back to life again. It was magic.

On the train ride home, my mother and I sat together, behind my grandparents. We were both very quiet.

"Do you have the soldier?" my mother asked.

"You mean *Sergeant Freddie*," I corrected and pulled him out of my pocket. "See? He's right here. I'm taking Freddie back to New York, and I'm going to keep him by my bed. I'm going to keep him forever, Mommy. Forever."

My mother touched my face gently. There were tears in her eyes. At the time I didn't understand why, because I felt good inside. Very, very good.

—*Pat Gallant*

The Reluctant Caroler

"Oh, come on, honey. It'll be fun," my husband, Jeff, pleaded.

"Yeah, Mommy, please go caroling with us," my three young daughters chimed in.

I stared gloomily out the window at the pouring rain. It was a miserable night, even for western Washington. Then I looked at my family's expectant faces.

"Oh, all right," I growled. "Maybe we can sing 'I'm Dreaming of a Dry Christmas.'"

Jeff hugged me, undaunted by my lack of enthusiasm. I felt more like staying home with Scrooge than caroling in the rain with our Bible study group. Directing two Christmas musicals on top of an endless round of shopping, programs, and parties had given me a bad case of the "bah humbug's."

By the time we met our group at a nearby trailer court, the rain was mixed with sleet. I gritted my teeth as the wind whipped the icy fragments into my face. No one else seemed to notice the weather, though, as they all called out cheery greetings to us.

We sloshed up to a brightly lit trailer, singing "We Wish You a Merry Christmas." The door opened a crack, but no one came out on the covered deck. Then, as we turned to leave, a silver-haired lady peeked out.

"Thanks for the carols," she said. "My neighbor was robbed last week, and I'm afraid to come out after dark."

The lady at the next trailer had no such apprehensions. She braved the freezing rain to applaud enthusiastically after each song. Afterward, she insisted we all come inside for cocoa and cookies. She seemed oblivious to the gallons of water we dripped on her floor. Her eyes were glued on the children as they gobbled down cookies. Her face glowed with pride as she showed us pictures of her own faraway grandkids.

By the time we left, I felt warmer in more ways than one.

We had started to pass by the next darkened trailer, when someone in our group called out, "Wait! I think I see Christmas lights inside."

We began singing "Silent Night," softly, in case the residents were asleep. The outside light came on, and an elderly man stepped out onto the covered porch to listen. I thought I saw tears glistening on his cheeks.

When the song ended, there was silence for a second. Then the man said, "That was beautiful. I wish my wife could hear you. She loves carols, but she—" His voice cracked and he cleared his throat. "She's got cancer and can't come out."

We stood stunned for a moment. Then someone suggested, "Why don't we try singing up on the porch?"

The man smiled for the first time—a little-boy grin that lit up his face. "Oh, that would be great! I'll leave the door open and go listen with her."

Somehow we all managed to cram onto the tiny porch. We sang "O Holy Night" through the open front door. Luciano Pavarotti would have cringed at some of the sour notes, but we didn't care. We were singing for the audience behind the door and for the audience above the rain clouds.

Several carols later, the man returned to the door with that little-boy grin still on his face. "She says to tell you thanks. It meant so much to her."

Impulsively, I asked, "Would you mind if we came in for a minute?"

My husband and children stared at me, almost as surprised as I was by my new attitude.

But the man acted as if twenty unexpected guests was an everyday and welcome event. "Of course, come on in," he said, motioning us into the tiny trailer.

I half expected to see a room full of gloom and darkness. We found the exact opposite. Yes, the frail woman propped up on the living-room couch was obviously very ill. But her eyes sparkled in her weathered face. Even the room seemed to reflect her joy. Christmas lights twinkled cheerfully on a tree, and the scent of cinnamon candles filled the room.

We asked a few questions and discovered they had four children scattered across the globe.

"Unfortunately, none of them can make it home for Christmas this year," she said. "Maybe next year."

I marveled at her ability to hope for joy next Christmas instead of dwelling on the pain of the present one. Then she told us of her two-year battle with bone cancer, which had ravaged most of her body. She brushed aside our expressions of sympathy.

"I'm not afraid," she declared. "I know where I'm going. As soon as I leave this old body, I'll be with my Lord Jesus." Then she sighed. "The hardest part is wondering which of us will go first."

Surprised, we looked at her husband.

"Congestive heart failure," he explained. "Doctors can't do anything for me." He took his wife's hand and smiled. "But that's okay. We don't want to be apart for long."

Before we left, several people promised to visit them and bring food on Christmas Day. Then we sang one last song: "Joy to the World!" The miracle I saw in that room reminded me of the one in Bethlehem—riches in the midst of poverty, joy in the midst of tears.

"Let every heart prepare Him room." I realized I had crammed so many things into my life during the last few weeks that I'd no longer had room for joy . . . and for my Savior. How could I have shut Him out, even for a second? I opened my heart wide to welcome Him back, and felt His love and peace flood in.

"Let heaven and nature sing." The joy welled up inside me and spilled out in music and praise.

Then, did I only imagine it, or did I really hear the angels sing along?

—*Teresa Olive*

Christmas Present

The first year following the breakup of my marriage seemed like a never-ending marathon of obstacles and soul searching. Each day challenged the tried and true approaches to a "normal" life. Living in this state was the mental equivalent of wearing brand-new, too-tight shoes. My whole life felt pinched.

The holidays were especially difficult. To my astonishment, Christmas came around again that first year after the divorce. I guess I'd thought, or hoped, the holiday would somehow just pass us by. How would we survive it? I was witnessing the disintegration of my family, first with the departure of our husband and dad, and now my daughter.

Our older daughter, Katie's, anger and distrust had surfaced prior to the divorce but had accelerated with alarming fury in the aftermath. Though the divorce settlement had been equitable, I had become the sole recipient of Katie's teenage angst.

Then, two weeks shy of her eighteenth birthday, Katie packed her bags and bailed. Simultaneously proclaiming her adulthood and her disdain for both of her parents, she loudly chose not to live with either her father or me. She stuffed away her dream to attend a fine-arts college along with her other childhood discards. Instead of wearing J. Crew and making the rounds of sorority rush parties, she donned a waitress uniform and moved into an awful apartment. Its barren rooms, stained bathroom fixtures, and broken front door seemed to reflect the pitiful state of our lives and our relationship. The tension between us had become so great I wondered whether she would even come home for Christmas.

My hope for the holiday was to preserve all of our family's traditions from past Christmases. I thought if we could re-create the past, the future would feel less frightening.

On Christmas Eve my parents, my sister and brother-in-law, my aunt, my younger daughter, Victoria, and I all gathered for dinner before attending midnight church service, as we had done on every Christmas Eve from the time my daughters were babies. We waited for Katie to arrive. She did not make the appointed hour. We waited some more. Eventually, we served the meal.

Katie finally showed up, cold and breathless. Her dilapidated car had died, and she'd walked several blocks in the freezing weather donned in heels and hose to join us. She sat at the opposite end of the table from me, never once speaking to me or looking in my direction. *Brrr.*

When it was time to leave for church, Katie, relishing the attentiveness of her aunt and uncle, rode in their car. Victoria and I followed in my car. After the service, Katie again got into the car with my sister and her husband. I assumed they were driving her back to my home, where I had planned for her to spend the night. But they never arrived.

I dialed my sister's home number; no answer. I dialed my mother; no answer. I became hysterical. It is uncanny how stress manipulates your power to reason. What could I have been imagining? That they had run off with her? Perhaps left her on the streets to walk back to her abandoned car? I have no idea what I was thinking at the time, but I remember exactly what I was feeling: distraught and fragile. Extremely fragile.

After what seemed to be endless pacing and ranting at the gods for stealing my hope for a warm, loving Christmas, my sister phoned. Katie had instructed them to take her back to her apartment.

How could Katie have preferred to be alone in a run-down, desolate apartment without family, tradition, or celebration of the season? Forget all those things—how could she choose to not be with me for Christmas? When had I become a human alienator? Did I repel everyone within my scope?

Numbly, I dialed Katie's number. I was greeted with a curt, "What do you want?"

"I want you here with us."

"Why?"

"Because there is no Christmas without you. Because I love you. Because I want the White girls to be together. Because there has been enough loss. Because I need you."

Silence.

Please, even polar ice caps melt.

Finally, she spoke. "Even if I agreed to come, I have no way to get there. My car is broken."

"Victoria and I will come for you."

"It's a one-hour round-trip and it's after one o'clock."

"Santa never sleeps."

I said goodbye and hung up before she had a chance to reply and ran over to Vicki, who was curled up on the couch in her nightgown, watching a Christmas video.

"Come on, sweetie," I said to Vicki. "We are loading up the sleigh and going to fetch our missing elf."

She wrapped her crocheted afghan around her to bundle up for the ride and off we went.

When we pulled into the back alley that served as a parking lot for Katie's building, I saw her leaning in a doorway trying to shelter herself from the wind. I wanted to scold her for being outside in the cold, alone in a crummy neighborhood so late at night, but I silenced myself when I saw her step out into the light. There stood my incredibly resilient child, clutching her tiny kitten in one hand and her overnight bag in the other. I opened the car door. Her greeting was dictatorial.

"I am not coming without Asriel. She does not want to spend Christmas alone."

My Katie, always putting up a fight, hurling conditions and qualifiers. She would never want to appear too easy. But I was not about to enter into a conflict over the sensibilities of bringing a kitten home with us, even though our elderly cat would have a hissy fit.

"Of course, honey, bring Asriel along."

My daughters huddled together in the backseat, sharing the afghan and cooing over a coal black puff of mewing fur. The three of us glided across the quiet, starlit highway.

When we arrived back at the house, Victoria drifted up to her bed in anticipation of coming down the stairs in a few hours to behold her bounty. Katie was not ready to retire and wanted to sit by the tree for a while. She turned on the Christmas movie that was still in the VCR. I was exhausted and wanted to do my Santa thing, so I could collapse in bed. I did not think I could outlast Katie, but I wanted to hold steadfast to the patterns of the past.

Every Christmas since Katie's birth, my husband and I had waited until the girls were snuggled in their beds on Christmas Eve before we placed gifts under the tree. We would carefully arrange their presents to create the perfect display to elicit a multitude of *oohs* and *aahs* as the girls tumbled into the room Christmas morning.

Out of nowhere, or perhaps from divine inspiration, I heard myself asking Katie if she would like to help me lay out Christmas. She studied me for a long minute, almost as if she were deciding whether to venture through an unmarked door, uncertain of where it would lead her. Then she bestowed upon me a miraculous gift; without commentary or debate, she simply said, "Yes."

That Christmas Eve, two women stuffed stockings, arranged packages under the tree, and waited peacefully for Christmas morning to dawn for their family of three.

—*Patty Swyden Sullivan*

Where the Heart Is

"Christy, go tell your brother and sisters to hurry up," Mom said.

"All right," I groaned. At nine years old, I found being the oldest child a gigantic burden.

I cupped my hands to round up my siblings, but Dad beat me to the punch. From the front door his voice boomed out, "Get a move on, kids. At the rate you're going, we won't get to Grandma's house until tomorrow."

Grandpa also lived there, but for some reason no one ever called it his house.

"Last one to the car's a rotten egg," Derris yelled over his shoulder as he ran outside, heading for the car.

Gari and Cynthia hollered, "Dibs on shotgun," and took off after him.

Being the family thinker, I lagged behind and

ended up squashed in the middle of the backseat. I elbowed my way to a comfortable position before Dad started the car and the chatter began. Try to imagine six people crunched in a compact car, everyone doing their darnedest to outtalk the others. No one got a word in edgewise, and most of the time it didn't matter anyway, because everyone only half listened to each other.

"I wish it would snow," said seven-year-old Cynthia, the family dreamer.

"Have you lost your mind?" I asked her. "It's eighty degrees today."

"So? It could snow." She made a face and stuck out her tongue.

"I wouldn't want that nasty thing in my mouth either," I said.

"Christy, you're the oldest," Dad reminded me. "You know better than to pick a fight."

See what I mean? I got blamed for everything, whether it was my fault or not.

Cynthia mouthed a silent, "Nah-nah-nah-nah-nah-nah," just about the time Mom's singsong voice resonated over the front seat. "Y'all better behave. Santa Claus might be listening."

Santa was definitely listening, since he was the one driving us to Grandma's.

Here's how I'd learned the truth: The year before on Christmas Eve, I got up in the middle of the night to use the bathroom and caught sight of Mom and Dad in the living room. One by one, Dad removed gifts from a huge department store bag and held them out to Mom, whose eyes sparkled like the lights on the Christmas tree. With every gift Dad handed her, Mom returned a tender smile before she turned to place the package under the tree.

From my hiding position behind the dining table, I watched in silence for some time and then tiptoed from the room back to my bed. I fell asleep feeling a little sad about Santa, but my heart felt happy, even though I wasn't quite sure why.

By the way, I never came clean about my discovery.

"What do you think Grandma will give us?" my brother asked from his lucky window position.

Mom twisted around in the seat and faced us. "I wonder." Her light blue eyes twinkled.

I'm sure she was kidding. A few days before, I'd heard her talking to Grandma on the telephone. She said, "I'll pick out something nice for the kids with the money that you sent, Momma." I think Grandma was much too old to go shopping, so Mom had to do it for her.

Gari squirmed around like a wiggly worm. "Are we almost there?" She was only four, so the thirty-five minute drive probably seemed like infinity to her.

Mom reached around to the backseat and patted

Gari's curly blond head. "It won't be long, honey."

"I hope Santa comes while we're gone." Derris's head was always in the clouds, just like Cynthia's, which made perfect sense. After all, they were twins.

Derris wanted a bicycle, but he was most likely going to be disappointed. Right after Thanksgiving I'd heard Dad tell Mom that he was working hard as he could just to scrape up enough money to buy food, much less Christmas presents. Mom looked like she was going to bust out crying. My heart ached seeing her so sad. I wanted to hug her and tell her I didn't care if she got me anything, but I didn't want to get in trouble for overhearing something not meant for my ears. Besides, I wouldn't have been telling the truth. What nine-year-old doesn't want presents?

"We're here," Dad called out. He stopped the car at the large two-story house where my mother and her five brothers and sisters had grown up.

We tore out of the car like it was on fire.

Grandma's front door was open and through the screen I could see loads of relatives inside. Many had spilled outdoors onto the huge front porch. A few swayed back and forth on the old white swing, some stood around talking, and others sat on the steps.

When we got close enough, they smothered us with kisses. After they said how much we kids had grown (what did they expect?), Mom steered us inside for more smooches. I suffered through, only because I knew I'd soon be able to play.

There were cousins galore in our family, and every year the numbers grew. I once mentioned how many new babies there were to my older cousin Danny. He told me the reason: "We're Czech Catholics and we do it for the pope." I had no idea what he meant, but he laughed like he'd told a great joke, and so did I, just like I'd gotten it.

Before long Grandma stood in the center of the dining room and announced it was time to eat. "Let's say the blessing," she said.

In unison we spoke the prayer we'd all learned at an early age. "Bless us, oh Lord, and these thy gifts which we are about to receive from thy bounty, through Christ, Our Lord. Amen."

Then everyone dove in. The dining table was loaded with turkey and dressing, Grandma's creamy vinegar green beans, salads, and homemade rolls. The buffet held pies, cakes, and cookies, and my favorite, *kolaches*. I jam-packed my plate with much more than I could possibly eat.

With a family of at least fifty, everyone took a seat wherever they could find one. I sat in a living-room chair and balanced the dinner plate on my lap. The cheerful voices, delicious food, and anticipation of the night's remaining Christmas Eve festivities made me tickled to be part of the huge family.

After dinner the aunts and married female cousins

cleaned up the dishes while the men chose the table where their favorite game would be played. From one table came the *clickity-clack* of "bones" being mixed up on the Formica top for a domino game. At another table, tall funny-looking cards from Czechoslovakia were shuffled for tarosy.

The kids took off outside to shoot firecrackers. The sun had set and the night air was so cold we were breathing smoke when we talked. About ten cousins, plus my siblings, were running around screaming and yelling. We were having more fun than a barrel of monkeys, until we were asked to come inside and sing Christmas carols. You could tell by the way the grownups' voices barreled out the melodies that this was the part they liked the best, even if most couldn't come close to carrying a tune.

After a jillion songs, someone saved us by saying it was time to open gifts. Some of the adults held gifts on their knees waiting for who knows what. All the kids ripped open their presents fast and showed them off to one another.

Grandpa, his hair as white as Cynthia's sought-after snow, sat in his chair and watched Grandma. Her apron was still tied around her plump middle as she passed out money envelopes to all their grown children, just like she does every single year. Regardless, they all acted real surprised at getting their twenty-five dollars. Mom and Dad were no different, except they looked at each other with what seemed like relief when they opened theirs.

When Grandma was down to the last packet of money, Grandpa jumped to his feet so fast it looked like a spider had bit him. His cheeks were rosy red and his blue eyes were cheerful, just as I imagined Santa's would be. If there was a Santa, that is.

Grandpa looked especially jolly as he watched several uncles bring in a box big enough for two people to fit in. The present was covered in at least three different wrapping paper designs and looked like the work of a toddler, but Grandpa stood proudly next to the package, like he was showing off the Vatican.

"Here, Minnie," Grandpa said. "Merry Christmas."

Grandma giggled and pressed her lips to Grandpa's cheek. He gave her a grin and then with a few fingertip brush strokes, he dusted off her kiss. He always did that. I told Mom once that Grandpa didn't like kisses, but she said he most certainly did too.

After Grandma tore the paper, someone handed her scissors and she sliced through the tape on the box and yanked the lid open. With both arms she reached in and pulled out shredded paper until it became a huge mound on the floor. We *oohed* and *aahed*. Grandpa had never done anything like this before, and we were curious as all get out.

Grandma just about disappeared into the box and looked like she'd fall in if she dug any deeper.

Then she whooped like she'd hit gold and rose up with two envelopes, which she held high in the air. We clapped and cheered. Her hands trembled as she slowly opened them. When she looked up at Grandpa, tears poured from her eyes.

"What is it?" we wanted to know.

Grandma lifted the corner of her flowered apron and dried the tears on her face. "It's been over thirty years since I've seen my sister. Grandpa has given me the airplane tickets and the money to go home to Czechoslovakia." The waterworks in her green eyes started up again.

The family was almost as excited as Grandma, and we showered her with hugs and congratulations. Her face glowed with happiness, and she kept looking back at Grandpa like he was an angel. He'd be busy wiping kisses aplenty off his face that night.

Soon it was time to leave and we said our good-byes. Cynthia, Derris, and I made our mad dash to the car for the sweet seats. It turned out the race wasn't necessary, because Mom declared that Cynthia and I got to sit by the windows on the way home.

Gari was sound asleep in Dad's arms. He positioned her in the middle, next to me. Her head slumped on my arm and I let it stay there. When her eyelids twitched and her lips curled in a little smile, I wondered what she was dreaming about. A few minutes later it got real quiet and I peered around her to see what Cynthia and Derris were doing. They were already in their own dreamland.

Poor Grandma, I thought. Even though my brother and sisters drove me crazy sometimes, I couldn't imagine going thirty days without seeing them, much less thirty years.

Except for soft snores and Dad's whispers to Mom, our ride home was silent. I watched as Mom scooted over next to Dad and he pulled her close. She pressed her lips to his cheek and then snuggled into his neck.

I curled up in the seat and rested my head on Gari's. Then I closed my eyes and hummed, "Santa Claus Is Coming to Town."

—*Christy Lanier-Attwood*

Love Needs Expression

I have a young adult daughter, Jill, who no longer remembers talking with her younger brother, Ricky. Yet, he was her constant companion from the time she was two until she was six years old.

By the time Jill was in kindergarten, we had moved five times and lived in three states. She made friends during the brief time we spent in each location, but Ricky was her best friend and she included her younger brother in almost everything she did. They rarely quarreled, and he was as much a part of her as one of her limbs until her sixth year. People who have lost a limb often say they can feel that limb after the loss. I know that Jill could feel Ricky's existence long after he'd drowned during a swim lesson in the city pool.

My husband, Chuck, and I learned much through our bereavement over Ricky's death, and Jill was often our teacher. Though each of us grieved differently, Jill mirrored our feelings to a large extent. Yet, she was the first one to express her feelings—and right to the point.

Her initial repetitive screaming of "I want Ricky back!" reflected our difficulty in grasping that he was really gone. The many transitions she'd experienced in moving so many times had been minor compared to the transition of becoming an only child.

She choked out that Ricky was getting more attention dead than she was alive, which was true. Our focus, subconsciously, was on our loss, not on what we still had left. She'd never been jealous of her brother while he was alive, and her directness alerted us to the void that needed to be filled. Often, we were too overwhelmed to nurture properly. Thankfully, new friends and neighbors spent time with her and took her places while we were incapacitated with sorrow.

After several months, Chuck and I started making a concerted effort to give Jill the support and attention she needed. We allowed her to sleep on a cot in our bedroom upstairs for a while, until she was ready to return to her own bedroom, which was on the lower level next to Ricky's. I helped out daily as a volunteer in her kindergarten class, mainly to keep an eye on her emotional state. She wasn't fooled as to why I was there. She would often come over to me and ask,

"How are you doing, Mommy?"

Despite our efforts to nurture our daughter, much of the time we were just going through the motions and doing what we felt was necessary. The depth of our loss was still too deep.

That first year after her brother's death, Jill never "fell off the horse." She didn't miss school the day of his funeral, and she didn't miss her swim lessons the week after. She didn't resist going on with these activities, so we felt it best to try to maintain her former routine.

We took for granted that she would voice her feelings and let her needs and feelings be known, which she was so much better at than we were. She asked many questions during that time, and we answered them as best we could.

Talking helped, and Jill was a good little communicator. Jill talked about Ricky with her closest new friends, who were our neighbors. The two girls had also known and played with Ricky.

That Christmas, just ten months after Ricky's death, we hung his stocking on the fireplace mantel. It was Jill's idea, and I'd hesitated at first, until I realized that it was her way of remembering her brother. It was also Jill's idea for the two girls next door and her to write memories of Ricky on pieces of paper and fill his stocking with them. The concept caught on, and family members far and near sent memories of Ricky to put in the stocking. Their expressions of love filled my heart as they did the stocking, and I no longer felt conflicted about seeing his stocking over the holidays.

Still, it seemed that holiday merriment and spiritual joy belonged to everyone but us. I struggled to appear cheerful, but it was all an act. My eyelids felt like sandbags from all the salty tears I shed in secret.

Jill would occasionally say, "I miss Ricky," but then she would put action to her words. When I was trying to come up with a positive way for our family to honor Ricky's life that Christmas, Jill suggested we buy some presents for Ricky but give them to someone else. She had enough money to buy him a slinky, she said.

I asked around and learned of a young boy named Seth who lived alone with his underemployed father. He had experienced the sting of death when his young mother had been killed in a car accident the previous year. With our mission at hand, Jill and I went shopping for the presents. Seth's father had granted us permission to secretly take Ricky's gifts and give them to his son. Jill and I bought a school bag, socks, a few toys that Jill thought Ricky would have liked, crayons, and a coloring book. I included a book that Ricky had enjoyed being read to him the previous four Christmas holidays.

Seth was alone and waiting for us when Jill and I

arrived at the one-bedroom apartment he shared with his father. His dad was working at a temp job that day. We made a little small talk, and then I asked him how old he was. Seth led us to an embroidered picture frame his mother had made, embellished with his birth date.

Jill said, "Look, Mom, his birthday is the same as Ricky's."

It was, right down to the same year. They had entered life on Earth on the very same day. Our minister once said, "Coincidence is the pseudonym God uses when He doesn't want to sign His name."

Just as Jill had lovingly shared her young life with her brother, she had opened her aching heart to spread some Christmas joy to another boy exactly Ricky's age. Through our six-year-old daughter's example, my husband and I had received a vital lesson in love and grief. In lifting the spirits of others, our sorrow was eased. Though Jill no longer remembers talking with her brother, I'll never forget that in expressing her grief and memories of him, she helped us to remember the precious gift we still had in our daughter and to let the spirit of Christmas heal our hearts.

—Helen E. Armstrong

Hanukkah Lights Bring Christmas Miracles

Twenty years ago, my Jewish husband and I purchased the first religious icon of our marriage at a flea market in Central Florida. It was a little crocheted chicken with straight white wings, a jet black beak, and a comb as red as a Santa Claus suit.

We were newlyweds at the time, visiting my Southern Methodist parents during the Christmas holidays. For nearly a week, we'd lounged in a home engulfed with twinkling lights, poinsettias, and angels, only to finally escape to a backwoods flea market that sold everything from life-size wooden reindeer to talking snowmen.

"Sorry," I told Bob. I was suddenly struck by a giant dose of what he calls Jewish guilt. "It's the third day of Hanukkah, and there's not a single Hanukkah decoration in sight."

I scanned the rows of wooden tables again, in

hopes I was wrong. "Look!" I called to him, spotting the chicken. "This could be our new tradition. Just like Santa Claus and Rudolph. We could have the Hanukkah Chicken. She could lay a gift for you on each of the eight nights of Hanukkah."

Bob is generally a quiet, tolerant man, and with a wedding band just beginning to feel comfortable on his finger, he was not inclined to argue.

"Sure," he said slowly, allowing the low r to slide into second base. "We can do that."

With that, the chicken dropped into a plastic handle sack and became part of our family.

Without even realizing it, we'd begun to nibble at the edges of a dilemma that Jewish-Christian couples face each December. Should we invent our own traditions? Mix our different traditions into some giant holiday fruitcake held together with matzoh meal? Make them separate but equal? Or just say no to one of them?

In a land where there are no perfect answers, we simply pondered the questions.

Our Jewish friends, having met The Chicken, weren't sure we'd pondered them long enough.

"What," they wanted to know, "will you do about the holidays if you have a child together? Then it will get complicated."

They looked wise as rabbis, stood back, and nodded their heads.

We didn't answer. This was the second marriage for both of us, and we were content to figure out one day at a time how to survive as a new stepfamily. We already had my sons James and Paul in tow. At ages five and nine, they thought the holiday problem was simple.

"Bob needs a Christmas stocking," said tall, dark-haired Paul, with the authority that goes with being oldest. "I know where to get one."

"Children's Palace!" cried James and ran to the car, blond hair poking wildly from his hooded red jacket. In the too-familiar wonderland of molded plastic toys, they knew just where to look.

"E.T.!" they gasped in unison, pointing to a fuzzy white sock that pictured their favorite space alien wearing a Santa hat. Paul snatched the stocking's little plastic hook from the display rack. "It's just perfect," he proclaimed. "Bob will love it."

Later, with glue and glitter, they wrote "B-O-B" in big messy letters right across the top and presented it to their Jewish stepfather.

"Like it?" James wanted to know, expectant as a child on Christmas Eve.

Bob felt the gritty letters on his new Christmas stocking.

"Sure," said the low, quiet voice, and he gave them a hug. With that and the Hanukkah Chicken delivering all eight nights, I figured we were set.

But after a year or so, Bob shed some of his newlywed reserve.

"Christmas is a holiday Christians have invented to punish themselves," he announced with exasperation one Christmas Eve. "Don't ever send me again to Children's Palace on the day before Christmas. There is no peace and love there."

"And I'm not comfortable with that wreath on the front door," he went on. "Or the tree in the picture window. I'm outnumbered, but the message is that the whole household is Christian."

My feelings were as mixed as the marriage.

"Now you tell me about the wreath," I said, "now that my fingers are itchy and swollen from making it. And it's a little late to be moving the tree."

But I also felt guilty. Guilty as the day I'd scoured the flea market tables in search of Hanukkah and come up with a chicken instead. The same desperate feeling that had grabbed for the chicken now reached for a new negotiated set of rules.

"How about a wreath but with gold ribbon only?" I proposed. "How about a tree inside, but not where you can see it from the street?"

"How about no lights outside the house?" he said. "How about never, ever sending me to Children's Palace again on Christmas Eve?"

It was with those rules in place that our daughter, Sarah, was born several years later, and we decided to raise her Jewish.

Our friends were right. The holidays did become more complicated then, but not in the way I'd expected. Suddenly, I—the Southern Methodist— grew more concerned about Jewish traditions. And Bob, not being a strictly observant Jew and not wanting to deprive his only child of the fun of Christmas, was eager to usher in the secular side of the holiday.

A Christmas stocking, he decided, was in order.

"How can we give her a Christmas stocking?" I wanted to know. "She would be confused."

"How can we not?" asked the owner of the E.T. stocking. "She would feel left out."

James went him one better. "Let's dress her in a Santa suit!" he squealed. "One of those baby ones with the little red hat."

Paul took him aside. "You can't do that," he whispered. "She's Jewish."

James gave him a knowing, confused look.

In a moment of inspiration, I decided the solution was a "Hanukkah stocking"—royal blue and decorated with felt cutouts of *dreidels*.

"I don't know why they don't sell these everywhere," I told Bob, proudly displaying my handiwork. "They solve a big problem. I could probably get rich selling them."

He just looked at me.

Soon, Sarah learned to talk—just so she could tell me what she thought of this not-quite-Hanukkah, not-quite-Christmas idea.

"Don't want!" she said. "Want red one with Santa."

My mother, who may have noticed that the "Baby's First Christmas" ornament she'd supplied was still not hanging from our tree, was happy to oblige with a bright red stocking covered with teddy bears.

"Christmas," she explained, "but not as much as Santa."

As time went on, we continued the struggle to bend without breaking, to melt together without losing ourselves. I ventured safely, tweaking my comfortable traditions with Jewish embellishments, trying to give equal time to both holidays, but always on my own turf.

One year, I tied bits of pastel satin ribbon and foil-wrapped Hanukkah coins to a miniature tree. Another, I tied toy dreidels to a wreath bedecked with gold ribbons.

It was not until Sarah grew older and began attending religious school that things started to change. She knew all about Hanukkah now, that there were eight candles on the menorah, that they were lit with a ninth, the *shamash,* and that every night there was to be a gift. She knew about the jelly donuts and potato pancakes (*latkes*) that made the holiday special.

"When are we making latkes?" she wanted to know. Her large brown eyes looked straight into mine, trusting that I could show her how.

"I've never made them," I confessed.

Her eyes were stormy.

"Then how can you teach me?" she asked.

"We'll learn together."

With that, we began to celebrate Hanukkah with Jewish traditions: shredding potatoes, squeezing out the liquid, tossing them with seasoned floor, and frying them in oil until they are golden brown. Peeling apples and steaming them into homemade applesauce. Lighting candles all eight nights.

And in our house, filling a huge wicker basket, set in a place as prominent as the Christmas tree, with a small gift for each night. All to celebrate the miracle of Hanukkah, when a day's supply of oil burned for eight days in a temple more than 2,000 years ago.

That is not to say that with the boys now grown and with more Jewish traditions in place we have completely resolved our December dilemma.

Sarah wants only Hanukkah gifts but keeps pushing for outdoor lights.

"No lights outside," says Bob.

"Outdoor lights mean Christmas," I say.

She argues like a lawyer. "Lights mean Hanukkah, too. How about blue ones or white ones? How about those candles in the window? We light candles at Hanukkah."

The debate continues, but since we found Hanukkah on its own terms, the season has been punctuated more by miracles than by strife.

One of those miracles is that by the time we'd learned to make latkes, we had lost the Hanukkah Chicken. Literally. That year, she simply disappeared as quickly as we'd found her.

I was not so sad about this. With the coming of the candles in the middle of my life, something unexpected happened. I had begun to prefer the peacefulness of a holiday that was symbolized by the lighting of candles and the gradual release of gifts, to the commercial Christmas blitz.

The real miracle may be that somehow, by finally finding Hanukkah on its own terms, I found the peace and love I had always sought in Christmas. These days, I find myself fighting to preserve the quiet of Hanukkah as a sort of Christmas gift to myself.

As for Sarah and her outdoor lights, I don't know the right answer. I am not sure there is one. But one thing is certain: Who am I, who once celebrated Hanukkah with a chicken, to say for sure that she is wrong?

—Pat Snyder

A Good Night's Dance

Christmas Eve comes early in the Northwest. Before three o'clock, Dad was searching the clear blue sky in the dimming of the setting sun. He frowned.

Though it might seem odd to some, seven children were gathered round and sitting or standing still, and not a one said a word. We knew better than to say anything.

"Where do you want it?" called Bryan.

Dad watched as Bryan and Jason carried the woodstove around the side of the house, and answered just as they came by the front porch, "Right there, on the sidewalk."

Bryan had helped Dad make the stove for our summer cabin. It didn't look too heavy, just sheet metal, but Bryan and Jason held it between them and carefully, slowly set it down. It was all done, ready to try out.

"A thing of beauty and a joy forever," Dad said as we all gazed upon it, but he didn't seem that excited about it.

I got up to go with Shaun to get some twigs and scraps of wood. As Shaun ran ahead, I looked back and saw Dad looking up again and looking worried.

I thought he was cheering up a little, as Jason lit the fire and we handed him bits of wood to feed it; as the smoke rose out of the stubby chimney; as we looked around, over, and under to find no cracks or holes. We gathered around, to marvel and to warm our hands and butts. But as the sun sank into the mountains in the cool blue evening, he looked all the more worried. *He might have to leave us now,* I thought.

I watched him watch nothing above, while the big kids—Jason, Bryan, and Lisa—went for some "real firewood." I knew, we all did, why he looked sad and worried, why he had to go soon. He and his crew had spent the whole shift the night before getting the buses ready. They had put chains on a hundred Seattle Transit buses. They had put sand in them, to dump in front of the wheels on the steep hills. There were a hundred buses ready to get people through the snow on Christmas Eve. And there was no snow. Dad would have to go to the bus barn, and he'd have to call in the crew, and they would have to take the chains off a hundred buses tonight.

The fire was going good now, smoke was pouring up from the stub of a chimney, and I thought the metal looked so hot it was starting to glow. Lisa looked around nervously, and I knew that she was thinking the neighbors must think we're nuts.

She worried about what people thought. She yelled at me last summer, "Don't lie around in the front yard! People will think we're a bunch of hillbillies!" But I didn't care; I liked to lie on the grass, to feel its cool greenness on my face, to close my eyes and dream. Sometimes I'd pretend I was asleep when I saw her coming, just to make her yell.

Getting warm, I turned my backside to the stove, remembering summer, and saw Dad coming across the walk. He wasn't frowning or smiling. He was . . . seeing . . . seeing something I didn't see, I thought. He stopped outside our little circle, put his hand to his mouth, and let out a whoop that made us all jump. I shivered, but not from the cold. Then he took a step and a hop, a step and a hop, and whooped again. Suddenly, I knew he was doing a dance—an Indian dance, that's what it was, and it could mean only one thing. A snow dance, yes!

He circled around and up and down, whooping and dancing, while Lisa yelled, "Daddy!" Then Lisa was gone, into the house to hide from the neighbors. And the dance went on. I looked up; it was dark, though the red over the mountains told that it was not yet night. And I saw clouds, not a few clouds or bank of clouds, but a whole sky covered over with storm clouds high in the cold air.

And then there were Bryan and Shaun, then Jason and Heather and Pat, and then me, dancing around the fire and whooping it up. And then there was snow! It came in big, fluffy white snowflakes, and it came faster and harder, and more and more came, sizzling on the hot stove and swirling around us until I couldn't see the other side of the street out front, and it piled up, and we stomped it down, and we danced on, until Dad suddenly stopped. Kids piled up behind him like a train with the brakes on, and we fell around him. He looked up and let the freezing snow land on his eyes and smiled.

"That oughta do it," he said. "Let's put out the fire and go in."

Our dad could do anything. And he'd be home with us all that Christmas Eve night.

—*James Robert Daniels*

"A Good Night's Dance" was first published in *Spring Hill Review*, January 2001.

The Christmas Well

When the city pipes broke at four above zero, the water spread out across our road like the thick roots of a crystal banyan tree and froze. We all came out to stare, our boots slipping on the remains of last week's snow. It was three days before Christmas. Our trees and lights were up, our cookies were in the canisters, and our stockings were on the mantel, but we had no water.

"Not until the twenty-eighth," the Forest Hills Water Department said and would have left it at that until someone got the brilliant idea of hauling up a water tank and putting it at the top of the hill.

"At least it's something," a neighbor said and went to organize her pots.

Others weren't so sure and said that the season was ruined.

Our community well arrived that afternoon. An

old World War II water tankard bristling with spigots, its camouflage shell looked odd against the neat prewar brick homes lined with hedges and crusted with old snow. Curious children and their parents watched a brief demonstration, and then were left to their imaginations as to how they would actually do it.

I heard about the tankard after I came home from junior high school. Mom, Dad, and my brother, John, had already carried enough pots of water into the kitchen to make it look like a battlefield after a major roof leak. (There was a leak of some sort, a family member later recalled. A pipe had snapped from the cold.) We had water in stew pots, canning pots, sauce pans, and even a few tin cans for the powder room. A large boiler was on the stove for doing dishes and washing hands.

In the living room behind the swinging kitchen doors, Handel played on the radio. The windows were painted with angels and snow, and the Christmas tree was ready to trim. Christmas was not going to be delayed.

Winters are cold and often snowy in Pittsburgh. Except for the hordes of children with whom I sledded in the open field below the alley, neighbors only glimpsed and waved at one another as they communally scraped ice or snow off windshields on the way to work or to shop. Snowman-worthy snow might bring out a few townspeople for a moment's divertissement, but that was usually reserved for the younger crowd. Most folks kept to their calendar of baking, Christmas-card writing, and package sending-off. Visiting applied only to a few close friends and often it was by telephone to catch up on the day's news. In winter we just stayed inside. The Christmas well changed that.

From morning to night we bundled up in our bright wool coats and scarves and rubber overboots and trudged up the hill to the tankard with our pails and pots in hand, like ants making lines to a picnic. Neighbors that we hadn't seen since summer or hardly knew at all tiptoed down their steep stairs or off their brick porches to go to the well. As we gathered at the spigots, conversations blossomed in the frigid air, puffing out like little smoke signals.

"What's news, Mrs. Hanna? Did you get your tree?"

"My car didn't start again."

"My grandkids are coming for Christmas Eve."

The pots and pans were filled, but so were the spaces between neighbors. Older times were recalled and strategies on hauling water offered.

"When I was growing up on the farm we had a pump. Had to prime it every time. Mother always kept a can of water next to it just for that."

"We had a well in Italy. The whole village used it."

We stopped and listened to the stories. We filled and hauled and laughed at our communal inconvenience. Our own village was born right there in our neighborhood.

Anything with a handle was employed. My family preferred our aluminum camping equipment, pots with wire handles that nestled together in the cellar when they weren't in use. But neighbors' containers ran the gambit of tin and copper pails to saucepans. Someone arrived with a wagon full of number five cans.

Techniques on catching water varied. Some hung the handle on the spigot and let the container fill until it looked too heavy to lift. Sometimes it was. Others held the handle of their pots until they began to tilt.

All day and night we came, the water spilling on our boots and onto the pavement. It was so cold that the water froze, leaving icy blobs around the tankard. At night under the streetlight, they gleamed like diamond cow pies.

On Christmas Eve day, the morning broke clear and cold, but by noon the sky had begun to grow flat. The wind stung our cheeks like a sharp wet kiss. We scurried for last-minute presents and lingered over the evening meal, wondering if it would snow. Would we get to church? Or would we have to stay home? Service at eleven o'clock in the evening was always an adventure.

Dark fell at four o'clock. We turned on the lights on our tree and in the windows. Outside, it began to snow. Invisible at first to the eye, the flakes grew from pinpoint to apple blossom size, sashaying down to the frozen ground. Bit by bit, crystal by crystal, the snow covered the street, the cars, the knobby roots of the oak tree in front of our house, with a tenuous mesh of white velvet fuzz.

Then, belying its gentle start, the snowfall suddenly exploded, throwing out snowflakes like the contents of a huge featherbed. In a silent rush, it covered everything and piled up, mutating the street into a close, distant world. By 5:30, it rose four inches deep with more to come.

"Janie, girl, will you go out and get water for dinner?"

I pulled back from the window and smiled at my mother, who stood at the swinging door leading from the long living room to the kitchen. She wore a Christmas apron with ruffles and her hands were covered in flour. Behind her wafted the smell of cinnamon.

"Sure."

I went into the kitchen and down to the side door landing where coats and boots collected. My mother handed me some pails. I opened the door and stepped out onto virgin snow.

In my life there are scenes that have stayed with me always. They are hallowed memories, forever magical in my mind.

Going to get water from the community well that Christmas Eve is one of them.

The world beyond was still and silent, and a

strange pale blue light reflected off hillocks of snow that looked for all their worth like confectioners' sugar.

My neighborhood had undergone a remarkable change. It no longer seemed an average residential street in a big city, but rather, a country lane in a long-ago time. The streets and yards had become one vast empty field, its hedges hidden somewhere under the snow. Candles flickered in windows. The trees overhead formed a tunnel whose roof was made of mist and falling snow. Far off, a street lamp beckoned like a muted star.

I tightened my mittened grip around the handles of the pails, and like a character from *A Christmas Carol*, went out to get water from the well.

When I reached the top of the street I stopped. Under a street lamp, the Christmas well stood, its cylinder shape topped off with several inches of snow, its tongue and wheels hidden. The bright yellow light of the lamp played over it and gave it a curious glow—like the manger in the Nativity scene under the star. It was impossible to see into the gloom around it. There was only the well and the snow rushing down from the sky. I felt utterly alone and at peace.

I put down my pails.

"Merry Christmas," a neighbor said as she peered around the other side of the well.

"And a Happy New Year," said another. "What a beautiful night."

From beyond the well, a line of scarves, hats, and coats dusted with downy snowflakes stepped forward with their pots and pails to say hello. My neighbors' faces were red with cold but each had that particular smile of goodwill and humor that had brought us to the well.

Christmas had come. A broken water pipe had not delayed it. We would gather our water and carry on with our lives as if nothing had happened. Except that something had. With each pot and pail of water we carried away, we also took a new sense of community and resourcefulness—and perhaps the true meaning of Christmas.

I live in the Northwest now, where we rarely get snow at Christmas. But each Christmas Eve, I think of that snowy night when I went to gather water at the Christmas well. As I turn on the lights in my windows and on the Christmas tree, I look outside at my tree-lined street to where a city light stands guard above the hedges. I don't even have to close my eyes to see the Christmas well glowing there under its light, the snow falling down on its cylindrical shape and the neighbors gathered around. It is etched forever in my mind.

Let us always be neighbors to one another, not only during the holiday season, but throughout the year.

—*Janet Lynn Oakley*

 King David

Dave took a swipe at his headdress and looked at the clock. The headdress was itchy and he felt squeezed, like a used tube of toothpaste. He loosened the cord of Dad's old bathrobe a notch and hoped he wouldn't trip over it. At least his old Nikes didn't show, except when he had to pull up the robe to walk onstage.

He looked at the clock again. He tried not to look at it, but his head kept swiveling around. They were really busy at the store, but she'd work it out. She said so.

Dave didn't want to be in the program, didn't want to be a king. Kings had singing parts. Miss Hixson went right on with it, anyway, and the first thing you knew, you were singing. That was the way she operated—on everything—on the whole fifth grade.

"I don't believe it!" Mom had said when she read

the invitation. "I've never heard you sing a note in your whole life. This I've got to hear!"

Dave didn't know he could sing, but Miss Hixson knew. She spoke to Mom and Dad at PTA and told them, "I do hope you'll be able to come. David does so well. You'll be proud of him."

Dad looked in his book and shook his head. "It's our last sales meeting of the year. I have to be there. I'm sorry."

Mom said she'd try . . . was the busiest time of the year at the store . . . same day as the company Christmas party . . . she was helping with the arrangements . . . she sure would try.

Dad told him that Mom would be named sales associate of the year, with a bonus. It was supposed to be a secret, but she knew.

Dave looked at the door, which was opening. It was just Rob's mom. Rob was Joseph. He didn't sing or talk—just stood around trying to look holy.

It was almost time. He was breathing a lot, which wasn't easy, with his heart crowded up there in his throat. He hoped he'd be okay when he got started. He swallowed.

Miss Hixson got up and welcomed everybody: mostly mothers, a few grandmothers, and a couple of fathers and announced the program. Then she sat down at the piano and played, "Oh, Little Town of Bethlehem," while Steve and Chris pulled the curtains open, real jerky.

The shepherds were there, kneeling by the crib, Keith scrounging around on his knees, knocking into Rob, who forgot he was holy and jabbed him one. The kids laughed.

Miss Hixson glared and shook her head. Then, nodding to the bathrobes, she launched into "We Three Kings" and they all stood up—like robots.

"Remember, you are kings. Be proud!"

Who was there to be proud for? Just that morning, she'd said she planned to be there.

Kevin started up and tripped over his bathrobe cord. He yanked it away from Dave's foot, hissing.

Kev grabbed up his robe and charged up the steps to the stage. Scott gave Dave a shove from behind.

When they got up there, Miss Hixson played the last stanza and started over at the beginning, with Kev, Scott, and Dave kind of straggling in after her. By "Oh-oh, star of wonder," they were together and sounding better. Louder, anyway.

"Let it spill right out," Miss Hixson said. "Sing from a full heart. From joy."

Yeah, right.

Kev had the first solo. "Born a king . . ." And he was off, eyes pinned on Miss Hixson, who nodded and smiled her PTA smile. Kev's mother was mouthing the words and nodding, but not smiling. Then they were into "Oh-ohh" again.

The door opened again. Mom! It wasn't.

Scott was next, blaring out, "Worship him, God on high." Scott's mom let her breath out on the "Ohh-ohhh."

The door stayed closed. And it was Dave's turn. He swallowed and started, a little late, but pretty much on key, anyhow: "Myrrh is mine . . ." His voice way off somewhere and shaky. Miss Hixson gave him one of those "Don't-blow-it-now" looks, and he gulped and quivered out, "Breathes a life of gathering gloom. . . ."

Miss Hixson nodded and smiled as he hustled on through "Sorrowing, sighing, bleeding, dying,/ Sealed in the stone-cold tomb." Another "Ohhh-ohhhh," the last verse, the last big "Ohhhh-ohhhhh," and they'd made it!

Kev and Scott looked at their mothers, who were grinning like cats. Miss H. gave the guys the "get lost" nod, and Dave hitched up his robe and dove for the steps, the other guys stumbling after him.

He slumped in his seat. His heart floundered for home past the lump in his throat. She'd get to her Christmas party for sure. Guess she couldn't do both. All he wanted now was to get out of the stupid robe, get that scratchy thing off his head, and just forget about kings, Christmas, the whole thing. Anyway, he wouldn't have to see this place again for two weeks.

After school Dave took out the trash and rode

over to Scott's on his old three-speed. He wanted a ten-speed, like Scott had. No use rushing home. Mom would be at her party. He was supposed to be home by six but why should he? Other people didn't show up when they were supposed to.

At 6:15, the phone rang and Scott told him it was his father, asking for him.

"Lucky you. I don't even know where my dad is."

"But the ten-speed—he gave it to you?"

"Musta been drunk." His lower lip stuck out.

That night, Scott and his Dad made sandwiches.

"How was the program? Was Mom able to get there?"

Dave shook his head.

"I know she'd have come if she could."

Dave nodded, trying to get the sandwich down—and said he guessed he'd go lie down awhile.

His father gave him a funny look and nodded. Dave lay down on his bed with a comic book, turned the pages for a bit; and then he was being held prisoner by robots—only he and he alone knew help was coming. He could hear the secret code. Tapping, tapping.

It went tappy-tap-tap again. The door opened a crack, and his mom whispered, "David . . . David."

He turned over with his back to her, faking sleep, and after a while the door closed. Now he was wide awake. Hungry. He thought about starving. Maybe dying. Then she'd be sorry. He wondered how long it would take him to starve. Too long, he decided, and tiptoed out to the kitchen. He could hear her talking in the living room.

". . . rat race today, but Joan said she'd handle it. I was in the restroom getting ready to leave when she got sick. I didn't know she was pregnant. I had to stay."

"Don't cry, darling, you couldn't help it. Dave will understand."

"When I . . . I . . . tried . . . just now . . . he turned his back. I came home the minute I could get away." Her voice sounded hiccupy.

"Your Christmas party. You didn't go? You'd been so looking forward to it, and your award . . ."

"I couldn't face it, just wanted to get home, to explain, so he'd know. . . . Oh, Jim! He sang. And I missed it!" She choked.

Dave found himself standing there, hand on the refrigerator door, filled with an urge that, for the moment, had nothing to do with food.

"Oh-ohh, star of wonder, star of night . . ."

He gave it the royal treatment. Not like a robot. Proud. Like a king. He gave it his all. From a full heart. From joy. Just spilled right out.

They clapped when he finished. Rushed in to hug him. Dave turned on the light and opened the fridge.

"What's to eat around here, Mom? I'm starving!"

—*Mary Helen Straker*

Love, Dad

"Yes, I am sure I'll be home on Christmas Eve. I'll be right here stuffing the turkey for dinner the next day," I answered.

This was the fourth time in so many days that my dad had asked if I would be home on Christmas Eve, and I was getting a little frustrated with his questioning.

My father was quite active for a seventy-nine-year-old. He lived in his own apartment, even if it was just one block away from me, and he drove his own vehicle. He had the typical physical ailments that anyone would have at his age, and he had gone downhill a little since my mother's death four years earlier. However, his mind and his memory were areas that were still strong, so I couldn't understand why he was so concerned with my whereabouts on Christmas Eve.

As an only child, I'd been very close to both of my parents during my growing-up years. My mother had quit her teaching job when I was born so that she could stay home and raise her family. Since she and I were always together, it was only natural that I should form a close bond with my mother. My dad, on the other hand, worked long hours, day and night, as an electrician in order to financially support our family, which prevented him from playing an active role in my daily life.

Because my father and I had to squeeze our love in whenever we could, my dad always made sure that the time we spent together was extra special. As a little girl, I remember a night when he came home from work and gently woke me from a sound sleep. With a twinkle in his eyes, he instructed me to open his lunchbox to look for a treasure that was inside. Imagine my excitement when my sleepy eyes realized the lunchbox was holding a small black-and-white kitten. I had been begging for weeks for a pet of my own. When a stray cat that had taken up residence on his job site delivered a litter of kittens, my dad decided that the smallest one of the bunch was going to be his little girl's companion.

As I grew older, I took on the role of tomboy and followed my dad everywhere, as he hunted and fished and took walks in the woods. On many a chilly morning I would wake at the crack of dawn to go duck hunting with him. We would sit quietly in the duck blind with our golden retriever, Rusty. While watching the sun rise over the pond, we would listen for the first group of ducks to land for their morning feeding. I never minded how cold it was, as long as I was crouching side by side with my dad, experiencing the dawn of a new day together.

In the summer, I spent hours sitting on the bridge near our house waiting with my dad for the perfect fish to take the bait from my fishing line. Even though patience is not a typical characteristic of a nine-year-old child, I would sit and wait . . . and wait . . . and wait, only because I was with my dad.

During these outdoor adventures, he also trained me to catch the slightest animal movement in the brush, to recognize different birds by their flash of color across the sky, and to treat all creatures in nature with love and respect.

Besides his love for animals, my dad was also a true genius when it came to gardening. He could recognize most plants by sight, flowers as well as trees, and he always knew which annuals or perennials would grow successfully in any garden. As an adult, it was never a surprise to discover that a container of pansies or a hanging basket of geraniums had materialized overnight on my porch steps.

It was his love for flowers and his love for me that brought us together one last time.

When the phone rang on Christmas Eve morning, I was expecting to hear my dad's voice asking what time he was to arrive for Christmas dinner. Instead, the manager of his apartment building, in a frantic voice, told me that my father had fallen in his apartment and the ambulance had taken him to a nearby hospital. She didn't have any specific details but was very concerned and thought I should go to the hospital immediately.

The drive there was like a dream, with everything moving in slow motion. Since my mother's death, my father and I had clung to one another like lost children, realizing that we were the remaining fragment of what had once been a complete family. What would I do if anything happened to him? How would I continue my life without his daily presence, his love, and his wisdom?

As I raced into the emergency room, I was told he had been rushed into surgery to try to repair an aneurysm on his aorta that had ruptured. It wasn't long before the surgeon came to me, put his arm around my shoulder, and told me he was sorry, there had been nothing he could do to save my father's life.

I was overwhelmed with grief and confusion, didn't know what to do next. I drove home as if in a fog, the short drive seeming long and surreal. The sky was gray and brooding, threatening snow. I felt as though the entire world was in mourning.

Walking into my house, I was struck with how dark and quiet and cold everything felt. The Christmas tree stood in the corner, but there was no twinkle to the ornaments now. An overwhelming impulse to crawl into bed and pull the comforter over my head gripped me. But instead I spent the next couple of hours calling family and friends, repeating the events of the morning, trying not to break down with each conversation.

When the doorbell interrupted my thoughts, I assumed it was one of the neighbors who had heard about my dad's death and was stopping by to give their condolences. Instead, I was surprised to see a delivery truck from the neighborhood florist. Amidst the holiday snowflakes, the driver got out of his truck and presented me with a long cardboard box tied with red and green ribbon. I thanked him and went inside to open the package.

Inside was a beautiful bouquet of flowers—carnations, chrysanthemums, and roses, all of my father's favorite flowers. Enclosed was a gift card in my father's handwriting:

> *Flowers for the most wonderful daughter in the world.*
> *I love you,*
> *Dad*

I suddenly realized that he had been planning this surprise for weeks and that his constant questioning had been his way of assuring that I would be there to receive his gift of a holiday bouquet on Christmas Eve. How could he have known it would be delivered three hours after his death?

As I sunk onto the porch steps and memories of all the wonderful Christmases and moments shared with my father flooded over me, I also realized that his last gift had come at the perfect time—assuring me that his greatest gift, his love, was never-ending and would always be with me.

—*Ann Downs*

 # Things

My family's Christmas ritual began early in
the morning, when my father went down-
stairs to set the stage while the rest of us waited in
gleeful anticipation in the upstairs hallway. It seemed
to take forever. We wanted to get to the stuff! We
wanted to run, screaming, into the living room and
tear into the pile of gleaming packages, amassing our
stash as the morning wore on. We wanted to acquire.

As it was, we waited lined up in order of size—
which was, at the time, also the order of our ages—
until we got the signal from Daddy. My youngest sister
stood on the first step, to be the first one into the
living room. Then came my brother, then me. Behind
me stood my big sister and then Mother—looking, for
some reason, as though she'd been up half the night.

The time my father spent downstairs alone setting up Christmas must have been delicious for him.

I can only imagine what he did down there during that torturous waiting period. I know he turned on the tree lights, and he probably put on a pot of coffee. Just to extend our wait he might have glanced at the television or put some finishing touches on his Christmas display. Whatever it was, he took his time at it. It may not have been more than a few minutes, but it felt like hours.

When he played Roger Williams's *Christmastime*, that was our cue. The opening strains of "Silent Night" were our green light, and down the stairs we'd run. Entering the living room was like entering the Emerald City of Oz, with piles of packages, colorful tree lights, and music overloading our senses.

For Daddy, it was more about the celebration he could provide for us than it was about the gifts themselves. To him, a gift needn't be fancy. He used to tell the story of his favorite childhood Christmas, the year he received the family hairbrush. He grew up on a desolate farm in western Kansas in the early years of the twentieth century, and his family was so poor that at Christmas they made gifts to each other of things they already had. They all used the same hairbrush, but for a whole year, he'd *owned* it.

That little farm boy who cherished an old, used brush became a college professor who loved his gin and wasn't home very much. At Christmas he invariably asked for socks, underwear, or handkerchiefs, which frustrated me to no end. I wanted to give him something special—something he would cherish, like the hairbrush. Something that would make him stay home more often, perhaps. But I never knew what that thing might be.

Every Christmas morning, Daddy would open his gifts and exclaim how wonderful they were. But they were socks, underwear, handkerchiefs—not exactly memorable stuff. No matter what we gave him, he said he loved it. But I always felt that I'd missed the mark. I wanted to get him a gift that mattered, and I couldn't figure out what that thing was.

For Christmas the year I was sixteen, Daddy gave me a pair of white gloves. They were the short, wrist-length kind that little girls wear to Sunday school. They had tiny flowers sewn on at the wrists, and they were very sweet. In fact, they were the sweetest things I'd ever seen. But I was sixteen and at the time I didn't know they were the sweetest things I'd ever seen. I was probably hoping for something "cool"— hot pants, or a Simon and Garfunkel album, or money—and Daddy had given me those dorky white gloves. I couldn't imagine what to do with them; I only knew I wouldn't be caught dead in them. They weren't even remotely hip.

I remember thinking, "Oh, my God, Daddy picked these out for me. He's so out of touch, he doesn't even know I'm too old for them."

But he did know.

I hunted through the box, hoping to find the receipt. When I happened to glance up, I looked across the blizzard of our family's Christmas chaos and saw Daddy watching for my reaction. He had a question in his eyes. He wanted to ask me something—or maybe tell me something. Our eyes met, and I held my breath for a second, but I couldn't bear the moment. Instead I gushed over the gloves, thanked him with a quick smile, and then tore into the next gift before he had a chance to say what was on his mind.

If I had spoken in that moment, I might have said, "Daddy, I'm growing up. Soon I'll be going away."

And he might have said, "I know. I just hate to see you go."

Things. You can touch things.

I don't remember what I did with those gloves. I probably put them in the Goodwill box as soon as I thought no one would notice. I never even tried them on.

Not long ago I was looking through a small box of things my father kept—his treasure box. There's a letter his mother wrote to him when he was in the service during World War II. In penciled longhand, she reports weather conditions on the farm. There's a little plastic box with a cartoon of an almost-naked girl painted on it—something a soldier would hold on to, I guess. There's a matchbook from a nightclub in San Francisco and the Bible my mother gave him when he went away to war in 1943.

And in my father's box of treasures there is a little tie clasp. It's handmade, with a W—his initial—crudely cut out of some kind of thin metal and stuck on crookedly with glue. It was made by a child's hands—my hands. I made it for him at summer camp, at least thirty-five years ago. It wasn't remotely hip. He couldn't possibly have worn it. But he kept it. He kept it.

—*Petrea Burchard*

Pure and Simple

"**H**ey, blue eyes! You're the best part of my day, know that?" Tyrone Williams looked up at Martha Bronner and grinned.

Checking his pulse, she flushed the least bit as he placed his free hand to his chest and fluttered his eyelids in a mock swoon. Not that there was any actual flirtation between them. He was an eighteen-year-old African American with an advanced case of AIDS; she was a diminutive sixty-year-old physician, Austrian-born, with large round eyes the color of blue topaz.

After twenty-five years in the United States, she still couldn't get used to it: the easy informality of Americans, the banter and kidding that erupted at the most unexpected times, in the least likely places. Austrian men in her time greeted women with *Kuss die Hand, gnadige Frau*—"I kiss your hand, gracious lady." Overdone at times, but courtly. Here at the County Aids Hospital, she never knew how a patient might greet her: "Blue eyes," "Tiny," even "Baby," terms of endearment from men who needed an outlet for affection, a way to lighten the yoke of fear that pressed on them like a sack of stones.

"So, what do you think, doc? Am I gonna make it?" Tyrone made an effort to raise himself on one elbow, searched Martha's face. Hoarse from the cough that worsened daily, he tried to sound jocund, but there was a desperate pleading in his eyes.

"Oh, you just might," she replied with a smile, lowering her gaze, pretending to study his chart.

He was the youngest patient on the men's ward. No, he wasn't going to make it. None of them was going to make it. But Tyrone Williams would likely be the first to die. Christmas was two months away. She doubted he would last beyond the New Year. At moments like these, Martha wished she had picked another specialty, anything other than pulmonary medicine.

He fell back on the pillow. "Wonder how my mama's doing," he murmured drowsily. He closed his eyes, drifted off.

It was the first time Martha had heard him mention his mother or any family member. Other patients had visitors, especially on Sundays, when they wheeled themselves to the solarium, clean-shaven, hair carefully brushed, a little flicker of anticipation in their lackluster eyes. They sat by the windows, where the sun's rays streaked across their faces. The disease had hollowed their cheeks, left track marks on their foreheads and around their mouths, prematurely furrowed.

No one visited Tyrone Williams. On his intake, "nearest relative" was listed as a grandmother who lived in Tennessee. His father was deceased; his mother's whereabouts unknown. When questioned about siblings, he had simply shrugged. Who would mourn him, the eighteen-year-old whose life, barely lived, was slipping away? With a heavy sigh, Martha rose and continued her morning rounds.

In the corridor, patients waved to her: "Morning, doc. How you doing? Me . . ." Their voices faltered. ". . . I'm doing okay, I guess." Some of them— Haitians, Creoles, Hispanics—spoke to her in broken English. Language differences were never an impediment to Martha; she could still connect with patients. The barrier she couldn't dismantle was broken spirits. She wished she could sprinkle hope, like a priest sprinkling holy water, from room to room, in every corner—the beds where they sweated and shivered, the bathrooms where they clenched their fists and sobbed, the solarium where in the presence of visitors they put up a good front.

Winter blustered in with scarcely a backward glance at the last autumn leaf that shuddered and fell to the ground. It was a week to Christmas, the holiday that each year Martha wished would hurry and be done with. The star-shaped cookies dusted with red and green sugar, the holiday punch, the roast turkey dinner, all left a bitter aftertaste. Dreading the new year, patients clung to the familiar one, clutched it for dear life. They feigned merriment, tossing jokes at one another across the corridor like Ping-Pong balls. Frightened children in the husks of grown men, they played "let's pretend." At Christmas Eve Mass, their veneer cracked and they unashamedly wept. Visits and gifts from family and friends cheered them a little: crisp, smartly tailored pajamas; hand-knit slippers; soft robes of every color and design—grim reminders of the fixed perimeters of their lives.

"Go ahead, put it on. No point in having it lie in a box forever," a stout woman said to a blond, fair-skinned man who was smoothing the folds of a plaid robe. His face turned ashen. There was no right thing to say at an AIDS hospital.

On Christmas morning, a line formed at the telephone booth. Martha knew that, even if Tyrone Williams had had the strength to sit up in a wheelchair and wait his turn, since no one ever called or came to see him, whom would he call? The hourglass of his life was rapidly emptying. She remembered his words, "I wonder how my mama's doing." His mother must be alive, then.

Martha went to his room, sat at his bedside. "Mr. Williams," she began gently, stroking his hand, the parchment-like skin purple-blotched from all the needles that had jabbed his veins. She never called patients by their first names, an American custom she thought disrespectful. "Mr. Williams, when was the last time you saw your mamma?"

He thought for a moment. "Four, five years ago, maybe." His voice trembled. "Before I messed up." He turned his face to the wall.

"Where did you see her?"

"Where? . . . Tennessee."

"Where your grandmother lives?"

"Where my mamma lives."

"But it states on your intake that you don't know where your mother lives."

He turned to face her. His expression was uncomprehending.

Martha was puzzled. After a moment, it dawned on her. She leaned forward. "Your grandmother . . . she's the person you call 'mamma'? She raised you?"

He nodded slowly.

Martha paused, then softly said, "She must love you very much."

He struggled against tears.

"What's her name, your mamma?"

"Stephens. Cora Mae Stephens."

She patted his hand and rose. "Don't let me hear that you haven't touched your dinner tray," she said, affecting a stern tone.

"Okay, baby," he murmured thickly, managing a feeble smile.

Later in her office, she pulled his file. His grandmother's name was on the intake: Cora Mae Stephens, Knoxville, Tennessee. There was a phone number. Martha jotted it down, tucked it into the pocket of her white coat.

Shortly after dinner she returned to his room, a phone in her hand. He was sleeping. Bending over him, she said, "Someone is waiting for a special Christmas gift from you, Mr. Williams."

Bewildered, he looked from Martha to the phone to the scrap of paper in her hand. She had begun to dial.

At the sound of a woman's voice at the other end, Martha tentatively asked, "Mrs. Stephens? Will you hold please?"

She placed the phone in his hand, folded his thin fingers over it. He held it as if he didn't know what to do with it.

"Tell me what I should say!" his eyes pleaded. His forehead glistened with beads of perspiration; his hand trembled.

Martha nodded at him with a reassuring smile, and then left the room. She shut the door behind her and stood outside. He wouldn't be long. He hadn't the strength.

When she came to his room on New Year's Day, Martha knew that he was moribund. Leaning over him, she placed the stethoscope to his chest. He groped for her free hand. She was glad she was there for him to hold on to in his last moments.

In a gesture that took her back a quarter of a century, a gesture that spanned two disparate cultures, two generations, two skin colors, he slowly brought her hand to his lips. There was nothing courtly about it, no flourishes, no bows. There was only love, pure and simple

—Bluma Schwarz

My Brothers' Keeper

For more than thirty years, to my family, Christmas has meant not a day of exchanging gifts and leisurely visits with loved ones, but a long day of work.

It is not that my siblings and I were not in a Christian family; we most certainly were, being the children of Reverend Hosea L. Williams, Sr., the founder of the Martin Luther King, Jr. People's Church of Love. In fact, three of my seven brothers and sisters have also taken on the title of minister at some point in their lives. And as children we did receive holiday gifts, lots of them. But usually not until a day or so after Christmas . . . depending on how long it took for us to clean up the aftermath of Christmas, the day we would join my father to feed the hungry.

From the day he walked through the streets of Atlanta with the mule-drawn wagon bearing the casket of his fallen comrade and friend, Dr. Martin Luther King, Jr., my father has strived to continue the King legacy in ways that he felt Dr. King had truly intended. It was my father who insisted that Dr. King's casket be carried by mule and wagon, the "symbol of the poor of this nation." After the funeral, he was compelled to follow the path that Dr. King had taken during the last year of his life: to advocate not only civil rights but also economic justice for all the nation's poor. He threw himself into organizing the Poor People's Campaign that Dr. King had initiated, and he served as the mayor of Resurrection City, when the campaign culminated in a temporary tent city on the Washington, D.C. Mall. Even that did not satisfy my father's heartfelt obligation to honor the principles that Dr. King wanted emphasized in his eulogy, as stated in his last sermon:

> *I'd like somebody to mention that day that Martin Luther King, Jr. tried to give his life serving others. I want you to be able to say that day that I did try in my life to feed the hungry and clothe those who were naked.*

Three years later, my father's search for a way to continue that legacy led him to a church basement, where he started the Williams family on a new tradition of serving dinner and giving gifts to homeless people on Christmas Day. Gone were our Christmas mornings of unwrapping gifts and our afternoons of large family dinners. He didn't always insist that we join him in "feeding the hungry," but we always knew he wanted us to—and that we should. We also knew that, regardless, there would be gifts from him, but not until the day after Christmas, after he'd been Santa for what grew to be thousands.

I remember one holiday when the Williams clan, including several grandchildren, stumbled over each other getting into the assortment of cars lining the semicircular driveway of the big family house and headed for South DeKalb Mall, black Atlanta's shopping mecca, for our day-after-Christmas shopping spree. We made our way to the designated meeting place, the mall Santa's now-deserted throne. Even if we hadn't arranged where to meet beforehand, all we would have had to do was follow the sound of his loud, raspy voice, charged with the passion that filled it when he spoke of things he believed in.

There was Daddy, surrounded by several admirers and curious onlookers, delivering his usual "You middle-class Negroes have got to realize that you are your brothers' keepers" sermon.

Hosea Williams loved people, and he loved to talk to people. I always said that all it took for him to get revved up was a pair of willing ears. He didn't care if the brain between those two ears was unwilling. He was sure that once he got going he was capable of enlightening even the most tightly closed mind.

The assembled group was delivered by our arrival. "Well, here's my family now! It has been lovely, lovely talking with you good folks. Y'all remember, you are your brother's keeper."

The dispersing crowd was replaced by the crowd of Williams children and grandchildren, all gathering around Daddy for our Kodak moment of family intimacy, in the middle of South DeKalb Mall.

"Now, everybody's gonna get their Christmas present from good ole Daddy and from good ole *Babu* (Swahili for grandfather), even y'all who didn't show up to feed the hungry yesterday. I guess I just ain't got to y'all yet," he concluded.

Digging deep into the pocket of his signature "freedom fighter" denim overalls to retrieve a roll of bills, he surveyed the group of assembled faces, seeing his reflection in each one, large and small. The wrinkles on his wide forehead, one of the characteristics we've all inherited, and the puzzled look on his fully bearded face seemed to say, *Where in the world did all of these younguns come from?*

But what he said was, "Y'all sure are a good-looking bunch of folk. You must all take after me."

After having a belly laugh over how funny he thought himself to be and showing how proud he was to be Daddy and Babu to his clan, he proceed to hand out the bills: a hundred to each of "the big kids"(the adults) and a fifty to each of "the little ones."

"Now, go get whatever you want. Just be back here in forty-five minutes so we can go eat and have a family meeting," he said.

Then he'd turn to look around the mall to spot who his next audience would be while we were shopping.

It wasn't the economy of after-Christmas sales or the efficiency of giving gifts to all of us at one time that compelled our father to use that public gathering to fill his Christmas gift obligations. It was simply that it was the only chance he had to give to his family during the holiday season. From Thanksgiving to Christmas, he worked nonstop, sleeping only during brief power naps, to feed the hungry and distribute food and gifts to the poor.

And the rest of us tried, but never quite managed, to keep up with him. It took a lot of time and energy to produce the annual organized chaos that resulted in enough turkeys, hams, dressing, sweet potatoes, vegetables, bread, desserts, and drinks to accommodate the thousands of men, women, and children who had come to depend on Reverend Williams for their all-you-can-eat, seven-course dinner—served with a generous helping of dignity—on Thanksgiving and again on Christmas. The wait staff was a small army of volunteers, some of whom came year after year to help with Hosea's Feed the Hungry and Homeless.

If you were homeless and ready to change your life that day, you could do it. My father had everything needed to get you headed in the right direction right there, right then.

No one would beleaguer you about it, though; the opportunity was there, but it was up to you to seize it. And if you did, you'd get a large plastic bag, much like Santa's, to fill at Hosea's "clothing center." From there, you could pick up a personal hygiene kit, hit the showers, and dress before getting your hair cut or shampooed and styled. After updating your exterior, you could renew yourself internally by signing up for spiritual and psychological counseling and medical and dental screenings. Then, if you were truly prepared for the final step, employment information and housing referrals were available. If not, you could still make a free phone call anywhere to someone who cared about you and might be wondering where you were on Christmas Day.

If nothing else, you could eat heartily, relax, enjoy the entertainment, and feel like you were part of something good. And you could watch Hosea Williams, the man who'd made it all possible, hand out toys and gifts, just like Santa, and fulfill his life-long promise to be his brothers' keeper.

That is how it was for three decades, since that first Christmas in 1969 when the Williams family and some friends served soup and corn bread to a hundred homeless men in a church basement.

In 2000, Reverend Hosea L. Williams, Sr. died of kidney cancer one week before Thanksgiving. Family, friends, officials, celebrities, and thousands of those he had helped or taught along the way gathered to celebrate his homecoming on a cold Tuesday afternoon. Two days later Hosea's Feed the Hungry and Homeless once again fed thousands on Thanksgiving and then again on Christmas Day. That year, rap artist Sean "Puffy" Combs and Arista Records president Antonio "L.A." Reid funded the dinners, and the volunteers included the governor of Georgia, the mayor of Atlanta, and Olympian Gail Devers.

Although my father didn't get the chance to feed the hungry in the new millennium, our family continues his work. Because in the twenty-first-century United States, the wealthiest and most technologically advanced country in the world, there are still millions of hungry and homeless people.

Now, when I think of my father and of all the people he nourished and nurtured over the years, I cannot imagine spending Christmas any other way. And though I might buy a few things before Christmas, I still like shopping the day after Christmas best. After all, I am my father's daughter and my brothers' keeper.

—*Barbara Williams Emerson*

 The Last, Best Gift

It was my twelfth Christmas and school had finally let out for the holidays. The kids on the bus were bouncing and laughing, showing off trinkets from class parties. When we got off at our stop, though, all joy drove away with our schoolmates, leaving us in a cloud of smelly exhaust on the long, empty road. We turned toward home to walk in single-file silence: five skinny, blond-haired, blue-eyed, look-alike kids.

Bits of wood flicked as Roddy, the oldest, whittled away at a little wooden warplane. Len, the youngest, stretched his stride to match Roddy's footprints. I watched Len's sodden shoelaces, flapping and frayed. Our sisters, Lis and Ellie, lagged behind as we slogged through the slush to face our first Christmas without Dad.

It was 1946. My friend, Quinn's, dad had died in

the war, and the ladies' society had brought special things for his family's Christmas. But not our dad, and not for our family.

In a way, though, it was the end of the war that killed him. He lost his job as custodian when the Baxter Army Hospital closed. After that, between his carpentry and our little go-broke farm, Mom said he just worked too hard and worried too much. We'd all stood there after the ambulance drove away, watching the snow whip across the porch light, feeling as bleak and hollow as that endless January night.

Then our own little war began.

Survival.

Come spring, Mom sold the farm, and we moved to five acres and an old one-room schoolhouse. We slept in an army tent, worked on neighboring farms, and spent every spare hour adding a kitchen and two bedrooms to the building.

Now the lights of our little house beckoned in the early dusk of Washington winter.

As we threw open the door and stomped the slush from our feet, Mom called, "There's a surprise when your chores are done."

Coming back from milking I saw it, propped behind the house—the most enormous Christmas tree ever.

We didn't question how it got there. Roddy and I wrestled it through the door. Its sharp fragrance penetrated our lungs as we nailed boards on and stood it up. Mom quietly fingered its deep green needles, which glistened from the melt of light fallen snow. Our eyes feasted on it. Its spike scraped the ceiling, and the branches almost blocked the doors to the bedrooms. Best of all, it crowded out the gloom that had followed us home.

Len ran in circles, whooping with delight.

Ellie begged, "Can we decorate tonight?"

Mom nodded. "If you can find the ornaments."

Ellie grabbed her coat from the school hooks by the door and dashed out with the flashlight, Len close behind.

"Try the big shed," Mom called. "And tie those shoes, Len."

The old farmhouse had been double the size of this little place, and we hadn't gotten rid of a thing. The two sheds and the old tent were pretty jam-packed, and the house, with its abundance of cubbyholes, was crammed. Everything was there, somewhere, but we could never find what we wanted when we needed it. Except for Dad's old carpentry tools, which I'd carefully oiled and hung in the smaller shed. I had a few tools of my own, one of which I'd found on the road last summer—a beautiful screwdriver with an oversized handle of inlaid wood. Dad would have liked it.

His tools were just about all he'd left to us. Those, and three end-rolls of paper he'd brought home way back when he was custodian at Sunset McKey Salesbook Company. Dad was supposed to toss them into the furnace to heat the building, but he just couldn't see burning a thing before its best use was realized.

They stood propped in the corner of the living room, two rolls of tissue paper and one heavier, good enough to draw on. I think that, until that moment, we'd been saving them, as if holding on to a piece of Dad himself.

Lis dragged out the heavy one. "Let's make a banner, Rich."

We cut a piece from the roll and smoothed it across the floor. As Lis poked through the stubs, she asked Mom, "Did you finish your Christmas sweater?"

"Mm-hmm." Mom smiled as she rocked and nodded.

Somebody had given her the yarn, and she'd been knitting every night for a month. We kids tried not to bicker and helped each other with homework, so as not to interrupt her. With Mom's new job on top of everything else, that Christmas sweater was the first thing she'd done just for herself since Dad had died.

Roddy joined the little kids in hunting for the decorations, and then we unpacked our memories— the tin carousel that turned in the heat of its candles, the old glass ornaments from Norway, the wooden crèche Dad had carved for us kids to paint, faded paper Santas from each child's kindergarten, and miles of crinkled tinsel and tangled lights.

It was the next day, Christmas Eve, before the last piece of tinsel went on. We fed more wood to the shiny porcelain Heatilator, and the room took on a glow all its own.

"Let's eat supper by the tree," Lis suggested.

"Like a picnic!" Ellie chimed in.

And we did. Hot dogs, macaroni, and green beans. With hard-boiled eggs from our own chickens, milk from our own cow, and ginger cookies we had all helped drizzle sugar frosting on.

It took forever for me to fall asleep. Roddy, next to me, didn't move a muscle after pulling up the quilts, but I could tell by his breathing that he was awake, too. Len rearranged the covers several times, but none of us spoke. Away from the warmth of the big room, the cold emptiness of Dad's absence enveloped us. He should have been tucking us in and closing the door with his traditional Christmas admonition, "You stay out of Santa's way, now. And no peeking!"

Nobody had even mentioned hanging stockings. We all knew Mom could afford only one small present for each of us. We all knew. But we weren't prepared for just how small that pile of presents would appear under that great huge tree when we crept out of our bedrooms in the morning.

The puddle under Mom's boots told us she'd already done our chores.

Ellie, Lis, Len, and I all scrunched on the couch and sat straight as pokers with our hands folded. The bentwood rocker creaked as Mom lowered herself into it. She pulled the hem of Dad's old blue corduroy robe around her ankles. I thought I saw tears in her eyes, but I wasn't sure.

"I'll stoke the fire again," Roddy said.

I think he was more intent on prolonging the gift opening than warming the room.

We all waited, trying not to stare at the base of the tree. I wished we kids hadn't drawn names.

Len's feet began to bounce in impatience. "Let Rich open my present first," he said, as Roddy took his place in the olive green overstuffed chair. Dad's chair.

Everybody said Len looked the most like Dad, but Roddy turned to Len with Dad's eyes and Dad's tone. "Hold your horses, sonny."

Dad had always started at the bottom of the pile so the first gift would be a surprise. But this pile was a single layer, so Roddy did the next best thing. He stirred them around with his hand to choose the first at random.

"Let's see here . . ." He turned the tag to read it.

For each gift, he stirred and drew, and slowly read the tag. But no matter how he tried to make it last, those presents were opened in no time at all, and we sat, each with two gifts in our hands. I held a paper ornament Len had made at school and a little pickup truck, real metal, with a red cab and a green box.

Lis got up first. She placed her gifts on her spot—"Don't anybody sit on these"—and knelt to look under the couch. Her bathrobe sleeve jammed way up as she stretched her arm underneath.

I couldn't tell what she pulled out, even though she was mere feet from me.

Ellie, who had a better view, got a funny look on her face. Then she, too, scooted off the cushion and left her presents behind to dig through the pile of mittens by the hooks. Then Lis hauled one of Dad's old tissue paper rolls into the girls' room.

Suddenly—it must have been magic, because I don't know how we knew—we were all looking for things, under furniture, behind boxes, and in cubbyholes, secreting what we found into the pockets and folds of our robes.

The second giant roll of tissue paper went to our bedroom, and scissors and tape were passed back and forth as we hid what we were wrapping from the others. With new gifts piled under the tree, we took our places again, not quite so poker-straight this time, and Roddy handed them around.

I unwrapped my long-lost penny whistle. Ellie hugged her missing baby doll. Mom had a matched pair of gloves again. We kept it up all morning.

We got dressed and searched the tent and shed, finding things, wrapping them, ripping them open again. We threw the paper every which way, bounced lost balls, tried on missing hats, played jacks. We got sillier and sillier.

We even sneaked into each other's drawers and wrapped things that hadn't been lost at all. Somewhere in there, Mom put cranberries on to boil and a chicken in the oven.

The aroma rose, filling the house. So did the mountain of crumpled tissue paper. We had to wade through it to get to the kitchen when she called us to eat, while the last set of gifts waited under the tree.

After dinner, I'd never felt so full. Not just of food, but of fun, of pure joy—and anticipation. I could hardly wait for the others to open what I had for them.

This last pile had more gifts than all the others. Roddy drew the nearest first and handed it to me. It was small but heavy. The scrawl read, "To Rich from Roddy."

My heart quickened, but I opened it slowly.

"Your best knife," I whispered. I was afraid I might cry.

The most magnificent magic had just begun, for

this time we had each sought gifts for the others from among our own treasures. My heart about burst watching Roddy open my screwdriver with the inlaid handle. Lis and Ellie ended up with each other's favorite dolls. I don't remember it all, but Len got two from everybody, because we each gave him our shoelaces.

As we sat amidst our bounty, eating Baby Jesus' birthday cake, Lis asked, "Why aren't you wearing your new sweater, Mom, your new Christmas sweater?"

Mom's eyes sparkled as she raised her eyebrows and said, "Maybe we're all wearing it. Maybe the whole room is wearing it." She rocked back and forth in the old bentwood rocker, her face glowing in the light of the splendid tree.

Roddy's jaw dropped; you could hear him suck in his breath.

"What?" said Lis.

"She traded it," Roddy said quietly, "for the tree."

All eyes turned to Mom.

"I couldn't have done it without all of you," Mom said. "Don't you remember being extra good so that I could finish on time?"

This time she didn't stop the tears in her eyes as we gathered around, hugging her all at once. And Dad was right there with us. In Len's face and Roddy's eyes, in the old blue robe, in the traditions and ornaments . . . and in that grand mound of tissue paper that had wrapped our Christmas and taught us the best use of things.

We hugged Mom until her chair almost rocked right over. Then we jumped and played in the paper like a pile of leaves. Finally, handfuls at a time, we wadded it up tight and tossed it into the shiny porcelain heater, watching the flames and feeling the warmth, one wad at a time, until they were gone.

It was my father's last, best gift.

—*Kathryn O. Umbarger, as told by Richard J. Olsen*

Kids, Casinos, and Christmas

Having had my first child when I was barely eighteen, my childhood Christmases segued into my adult ones almost seamlessly and were spent the same way as far back as I remember. Christmas Eve we visited with family, the night stretching into the wee hours of the big day. Then, long before the sun had risen, the house would slowly come to life. Partly from exhaustion, partly from excitement, the butterflies in my stomach would swing into high gear as we gathered in the living room to see what Santa and Grandma had brought.

This year, Santa didn't come on Christmas morning.

For ten years, I had watched my daughters do the same things my brother and I had done: creep cautiously out of their bedrooms, peeking around the corner to see if Santa had come. Come in to wake the parents, gently at first, then more insistently. Finally, the whole family assembled in the living room, we'd tear paper off packages, the room ringing with shouts of, "Hey, cool! Just what I wanted!"

This year, I dreaded Christmas, because this year, it wasn't my turn. The year prior, I'd readily agreed when the lawyer had said, "Alternating years, the girls will spend Christmas with their father." At that point, Christmas apart was a whole year away. A year never flew by so quickly, and now there would be nothing but silence on Christmas morning.

Selfishly, I tried to convince the girls' father to alter the plan. My parents had divorced when I was eight; Christmas was always with Mom and Mom's family. Dad would come on Christmas night and bring us to his house, where we'd celebrate the holiday on Boxing Day. If my father had a problem with the arrangement, he'd never indicated it to me; it was simply the way things were.

But their dad was entitled to his Christmas, so I put on a brave face for the girls, assuring them that we'd have our Christmas on Boxing Day. My extended family had agreed to have our big family dinner all over again then, so that we could include my daughters. There was an unexpected perk: my brother's daughter, five-year-old Kaitlyn, would be part of the family celebration this year. Like me as a child, Christmas Day belonged to Kaitlyn's mother.

But my Christmas would be childless, for the first time ever. I couldn't contemplate a Christmas celebration without children present, couldn't imagine what adults might do with the day without children around.

From difficult situations, creative solutions arise. A week before Christmas, my father called—my father, who'd been apart from his children on Christmas morning for many years. My teenaged half-siblings were spending Christmas with their mom. My mother, my brother, and I would all be alone when the sun rose on December 25. Why not do something different?

And so, my father offered a gift: two hotel rooms at Windsor Casino on Christmas Eve—one for my mother and me, the other for him and my brother.

I felt awkward just envisioning it. Since my brother and I had attained adulthood, my parents hadn't interacted much. If anything would distract me from missing my girls, I figured this had to be it. I might even win at the quarter slots.

For the first time in twenty-one years, the four of us sat at the same table and shared a meal. After supper on Christmas Eve, we wandered our separate ways and met again for breakfast. As I stared across the table at my brother on Christmas morning, the two of us exchanged a look of incredulity, tempered with a feeling of nostalgia. It wasn't the Christmas of our childhood with stockings and wrapping paper, but this was our family and we were together again.

We'd come together to keep each other company on what otherwise would have been a lonely day for all of us. I don't know whether my parents will ever realize what they did for us that day; they'd reminded us that we could always count on our parents, married or not.

I learned a few things this Christmas: That the time I spend with my children is precious, not only on holidays but always, because it is never guaranteed. That families come in all shapes and sizes, a platitude I'd spoken often but never truly grasped. That divorce doesn't have to destroy a family. And that Christmas can be celebrated any way and anywhere, with or without children, as long as love, peace, and goodwill prevail.

—*Shelley Divnich Haggert*

Just a Little Extra

I grew up on a small farm in southern Indiana. What little money my father earned was spread thin by the time it provided for seven people, which included two grandparents and an uncle, as well as the livestock and the ramshackle machinery he perpetually patched together in order to farm.

In the winter when everything froze hard outside, my sister and I slept on pallets in the living room because the linoleum on our bedroom floor iced over. We took a bath together at night in a tub filled with just enough water to graze the back, because the stock took priority and our parents lived in constant worry that the well would run dry; of course, we didn't even have indoor plumbing until I was almost four. I didn't watch a television set until I was in the third grade, and the only time I ate oranges was at Christmas.

My family was not unique, however. Our whole community, all of the people living in all of the farmhouses that dotted the fields of soybeans and corn and rye and winter wheat for as far as the eye could see across the softly rolling landscape, were in a similar economic situation. Things were tight all over.

Still, when our neighbors' hay barn burned down during a lightening storm one spring night, I stood on a stool beside my grandmother and sister in the kitchen and watched farm truck after farm truck, the rest of my family in one of them, flood up the long drive to the huge barn. People came from all around to help rescue the horses and cattle, the tractors and wagons, whatever they could before the hand-hewn beams of the two-story structure collapsed in a roar of white-hot flames. For days afterward, I watched those same trucks deliver odds and ends of building materials, hay, grain, even animals to replace the ones lost.

Months later on the Sunday before Christmas, with those neighbors who'd lost their barn still on the thin edge of recovery, I overheard the quiet voices of my mother and grandmothers and the women of our little country church as they planned for "just a little extra" in their food preparations and the gifts they had made or bought. I knew who they meant, even though I don't recall them ever saying directly, just as I knew when I overheard my father and grandfathers talking with the other men about straw and hay and feed and firewood that they meant to help the same folks.

Throughout my growing-up years, every time a house burned down, every time someone fell ill or, worse, died, every time calamity struck anyone in our little rural community, it was met fully, swiftly, and wholeheartedly by everyone else. No one went hungry or cold or homeless. No one. Service wasn't something people did for a line on a resume; it wasn't something done to brag or show off about; there was no grandstanding, no trying to outdo one another. If there was a need, it was met to the best of the community's ability, period. It was simply a regular part of everyday life.

One Christmas Eve twenty-some years later, when my two older children were small and our family was suffering some tough financial times, we learned through the grapevine of a woman in a small town a few miles away who had nothing to give her own children the next morning. As I began to sort through the fruit and baked goods, all the preparations that we'd made for our Christmas dinner, my husband called the kids into the kitchen to explain the situation and ask if they would like to help. They scurried around the room in their footed pajamas and robes, adding one more orange, another can of green beans, two more pieces of homemade candy to the box, whatever they considered important to include.

As I closed the lid on the food box, they asked about the woman's children, if they were boys or girls, how old they were. My husband and I told them that there was a girl and a boy, about their same ages.

"What about toys?" they wanted to know. "Would the children get any toys on Christmas morning? Would Santa find them if they had no cookies and milk to set out?"

"Santa could probably use some help," we said.

And we waited, watching their faces, watching the wheels spin in their heads.

And then they did an amazing thing.

Without a word, our little boy and little girl went to the Christmas tree and selected from beneath it the present they each wanted most—because kids always know what's in every box no matter how hard you try to disguise it—and they brought the gifts to the table and placed them beside the box of food. Our daughter offered the Barbie doll she'd waited on for months; our son his big Tonka truck, equally anticipated. It was difficult for them to actually let go of the gifts, they had wanted them for so long and knew, too, that it would be awhile, maybe months, before replacements would arrive. But after they'd managed to lift their hands fully away from the boxes, they turned back to the tree for another gift, one they had wrapped themselves: the house slippers they had paid for with their meager allowances, their gift to me.

"This way," they said, "everyone including the mommy could have a present. That would be okay with you, Mommy, wouldn't it?"

Our children are grown now, and every year as part of our family holiday tradition, we select a local organization or a family who is experiencing hard times and donate our goods or services. We make trips to the Humane Society with pet food, cleaning supplies, copy paper, or blankets for the animals to call their own while they wait for real homes. We bake pies and cakes for days ahead to deliver to the Rescue Mission for the hundreds of homeless men, mostly veterans, whose hearts need the comfort of homemade food as much as their bodies need clothing. We select families burdened by medical bills or unemployment and buy toys and school clothes for each child as well as food for the family. Whatever we choose to do, we do it together.

One year not so long ago our family was heart-heavy with sadness from a relative's tragic death. No one wanted to shop for gifts or decorate the tree and house. No one wanted to bake or visit with neighbors, not even talk among ourselves, really. Even Christmas music on the radio seemed an affront. Out of habit, I think, midafternoon on Christmas Eve,

I picked up the phone book, ran down the Yellow Pages, stopped on the number for a local shelter for abused women and children, and dialed. I asked the receptionist how many women and children were lodged there for the night, the ages and sexes of the children, and how late it would be possible to enter the building. The woman sounded hesitant, so I reassured her that I was asking so my family could bring donations.

We left the house early enough to allow for shopping and delivery but still arrive on time for our extended family celebration across town. We went to a discount store chain, because most stores were already closed for the holiday and we had a variety of items to buy.

Five women and thirteen children, infant to adolescent, were calling the second floor of the shelter home for Christmas. As soon as we entered the store, I tore the list in sections to divide among us, and as we scattered in hot pursuit of appropriate gifts, I thought how lucky I was to have bills to worry over, work to exhaust me, a house to fuss about cleaning and repairing, and especially my husband and children. I thought about how fragile we are, how fragile the world is, and how sometimes we need each other just to survive and always to truly live.

Within a brief time, as if all on the same clock, we rounded to the front of the store, gifts in hand.

My husband had the babies on his part of the list, and he had chosen warm, soft clothing and pacifiers in pinks and blues. My daughters carried Barbie dolls and baby dolls and stuffed kitties and puppies for the little girls. I had house slippers for each of the mothers. But my son was the one who came back with the one gift that drove the whole point home.

On his list was the eleven-year-old, a boy, the toughest gift to choose. And when my son held out his selection, I hesitated before offering my agreement as I had for the others.

"Just feel it," my son insisted, handing me the bright blue, fake fur football. "It's soft like a stuffed toy, so he can sleep with it and hold on to it for comfort, but it's a football, so he can still look tough and not have to be embarrassed."

"It's perfect," I said, "just perfect. How did you get so smart?"

We bought the wrapping paper and bows and tape, some boxed cookies and candies, several bags of oranges, and the gifts. We wrapped the gifts in the car; then we all went into the shelter together, arms full, and asked a dumbfounded receptionist where to put the items. For a minute she couldn't even answer, then waving us to a side door, she called to the other women working regular shifts that happened to fall on Christmas Eve to come look.

As we stacked the sacks and boxes on the floor

inside the tiny office, I explained which gifts were intended for which children, that the house shoes were for the moms, and that the food was for everyone, including the staff workers. My husband signed a form verifying we had donated the items, and we all thanked them for their good work, wished them a happy holiday, and turned to leave. Then the woman who had answered the phone told me she had expected cookies or a pie and that she'd thought at the time how nice it was for someone to think of the women and children driven by terrible circumstances to spend the holidays there. She had never expected, or seen, she'd said, anyone bring actual gifts for Christmas. All I could wonder as we left was, *Why not?*

Later that evening in a house filled with the aroma of good food and the sounds of music and games, even laughter, I sat content and warm in front of the fireplace. I could hear my family all around me, safe and happy in that moment. I knew the money we had spent would mean no trips to the video store for a while, no junk food at the grocery store, maybe even that we would turn the thermostat down for the next month.

But as I watched the fire jump and hiss in the fireplace, I saw again in my memory that old barn. Flames shot up and roared against the black sky, but piece by piece by piece, help came in the shape of neighbors, weaving with their generosity of spirit a net beneath the ones among them in need.

Most of those good folks are dead now, including many of my own relatives. But nothing touches me more in this world than when I see in someone else the same kindness and caring I once saw demonstrated in them. And that is what I have tried to live by and to pass on. The only true moment of Christmas is the one when you hold out your hands—to give. It takes so little really, just a little extra time, a little extra effort, almost nothing at all, when you think about it.

—*Leisa Belleau*

A Child Shall Lead Them

As grandmother and narrator, I was in charge. Or so I thought.

On the morning of Christmas Eve, I had all five of my grandchildren with me as their parents did last-minute shopping and Grandpa stacked wood. Their teenage uncle, Brian, helped me keep everyone occupied. Brad and Tyson sorted gumdrops for gingerbread cookies. Amy and Bridget plunked out carols on the piano. Shannon, the fiesty youngest, elbowed her way to the frosting bowl.

Earlier in the week, we had enjoyed the Sunday school pageant, gone caroling on a decorated hay truck, and made ornaments and candles for gifts. This was our "home" day, warm and filled with Christmas sounds and smells.

Looking at Shannon, with red frosting smeared over her face and arms, I said, "Let's plan a pageant.

Right here. Shannon, would you like to be Mary?"

Her eyes twinkled as she ran into my arms. "Yes, Grandma, yes! Can I get the costume box?"

While Shannon poured through yardage, the rest of us finished decorating cookies, decided which child would play which part, and collected candles and greens for the program. Their parents, grandpa, and great-grandma would be the audience.

Brad pulled on an old wig and a pageant-weary jeweled crown, while Tyson dressed in brown burlap as Joseph. Amy and Bridget tied garlands in each other's hair and pranced around the living room flapping their wings with angelic secrets in their smiles. Brian donned the costume of the innkeeper and took charge of the music.

Shannon stopped wiggling and calmed down as I draped her in yards of blue cotton. Her eyes softened as her lips brushed the cheeks of the doll that would be baby Jesus. A holy kind of hush engulfed us as we watched her cradle the face of the baby Jesus and hum softly in his ear.

"Okay, kids, let's begin." I opened my Bible and read: *"Mary and Joseph traveled from Nazareth to Bethlehem to be taxed."*

I patted Shannon's shoulder. "Walk with Tyson, honey. Remember, you're tired from a long journey."

Brian turned up the cassette player as they walked toward the simple Nativity scene we had created.

"O Little Town of Bethlehem" reached out to my memories of the Christmas pageants of my own childhood. The purity in the children's voices reflected the heart and true meaning of Christmas. I could see on their faces that they, too, felt the wonder.

Brian, our innkeeper, stood tall and persuasive. "There's no room for you here," he said sternly.

Mist glazed Shannon's eyes as I continued the scripture: "... *because there was no room for them in the inn.*"

Suddenly, she stormed out of the room, returning with her favorite threadbare blanket.

"There is too room, Grandma!" she bellowed, as she stood her ground with hands on her hips. Then she picked up the babe, propped in the manger, wrapped him carefully, snuggling his head under her chin, and carried him back to her bed.

We all stood there, looking at each other. Shannon had taken the Christ child into her arms and into her heart, and shown us the simplicity and wonder of accepting His grace.

Wind rustled the patio chimes; candlelight danced across damp evergreens and the empty manger. Surprise on our faces must have been like the awe of those long-ago participants at Jesus' birth. Christmas had come. And we all burst into song:

"*O, come let us adore Him!*"

—*Doris Hays Northstrom*

Star of Wonder

The darkness, though encompassing, was anything but quiet and still. Three little figures
bounced along in front of me, flashlight beams jerking
spastically around, revealing split-second images: fen-
cepost, pasture, dirt, packed clay, yellow coat, green
cap. My husband reached over and held my cold hand
in his large, warm one. He squeezed once to let me
know he was aware of my gloomy mood.

I stepped up my pace, determined to outdistance
the shadow of sadness that followed me, so as to
share in the joy of my family's winter ritual. This was
the night of our "cold walk."

It was a perfect night, really. Rarely in our South
Texas climate does the first cold night of the season
happen to hit on the night we first turn on our
Christmas lights. But on this night it had happened.
We were able to take our cold walk with the added

bonus of viewing our Christmas lights from a distance.

After a long, extremely hot summer and a short indistinguishable fall, the first cold front to blast across Texas is a noticeable event. There are some who say we don't have a true change of seasons in South Texas, but with or without leaves in various shades of red, when an icy wind slaps you in the face immediately on the tail of a warm southern breeze, you'd better believe you notice it.

When I was a child, my father had celebrated this exciting change in the weather with a cold walk. After a summer and fall spent in shorts and sandals, my sister and I were awkwardly bundled up in our some-what foreign coats and hats. We then headed out into the darkness, leaving our mother behind to stir up some hot cocoa with which to welcome us home.

We'd walk with our dad, basking in the shocking chill that we knew could very well be gone by the next day, replaced again by balmy air. Over the years, we spent many a Christmas Eve with our windows open and fans whirring, so we cherished this bit of winter and secretly hoped for a Christmas where we wouldn't wilt beneath our brand-new sweaters.

As we took our cold walk with Dad, my sister and I would watch our long shadows and puff our frosty breath. It was a little bit scary out there in the dark, and a whole lot of fun. We'd walk until our noses stung and our fingers grew numb and slipped from the mittens grasped by our father's strong hands. We wanted the walk to last forever, and at the same time, we couldn't wait for it to end so we could rush back to the warmth of our house and our mother's arms.

I let my mind linger on the sweet memories of my childhood as I walked down our farm's dirt lane with my husband and children, walking briskly to warm myself in the bracing air. Yet, I found myself trying to shake off more than the chill. I was trying to shake off the overwhelming feeling of sadness I had carried home from a visit with my parents, earlier in the day.

The usual excitement of the Christmas season was painfully absent from their house. There had been no tree. There had been no lights. My dad had tried to welcome me with a hug, but his fatigue was so great that he could barely manage a smile. His shoulders were as full as my mother's eyes were empty. Rather than Christmas cheer filling the air, it was shrouded in the darkness and gloom of Alzheimer's disease.

I had hoped that, somehow, the magic of Christmas would have found its way into my childhood home. But it had not. Christmas had forgotten my parents. My parents had forgotten Christmas. I felt forgotten, as well. Forgotten by my mother who didn't remember my name, and worse, forgotten by God.

I had stayed and helped my dad, who suffered the very hard work of being a lone caregiver. I had done the best I could to lighten his load, but as I left I had the usual feeling that nothing had changed. Nothing I had been able to do during my visit seemed to matter much in the grander scheme of things. I could not bring the light back to my mother's eyes, and I missed the warmth of her arms.

Now, outside in the cold, surrounded by my elated children, I gave my shoulders one last shake and quickened my step. I was determined to take my own youngsters on a cold walk they'd always remember.

The sky was bright with stars, crisp and clear, and little voices cut through the air with shrieks of delight. The children watched their breath and gazed in delight from beneath knit caps at the frigid night world while trying to hold on to flashlights with mitten-clad hands.

As I walked, I felt the shadow of sadness falling farther behind. The bite of the cold air against my face woke me up to the joy of the night, and of the moment. As we arrived at the very end of our long dirt lane, right where it meets up with a longer dirt road, we prepared to turn around and head back. But just before we could, we saw a spectacular thing: A beautiful falling star, red and flaming with a huge sparkling tail, blazed across the sky.

We stood speechless as it lit up our night—and literally shot from end to end of the sky, staying visible for several seconds. Shocked silence quickly gave way to hoops and hollers of excitement as the children realized what they'd seen: their first falling star. What a sign!

As we headed home, I felt my burden lift and a sense of peace envelop me. My husband was equally excited, intrigued by how close we'd come to missing it completely. Could I believe that they were all three looking? Could I believe it happened just before we turned around? The timing, he thought, was accidentally perfect.

But I felt there was no way we would have missed that star. It was our star, meant especially for us. I could almost hear a voice say, *I haven't forgotten you. I see you down there in the darkness. I hear your joyful cries. And I hear your painful pleas. I was just waiting until you were looking to answer.*

We walked home quietly, the shadow of sadness replaced with something else. Not hope, really. More like . . . reassurance.

The comforting feeling followed us back down our dark country lane, made crisp and cold by a burst of wind from the north. Back to our small and plain house, made somehow spectacular by a row of colored lights, shining bright in a dark pasture. Back to warmth, our hearts renewed by a falling star that carried a very special Christmas message:

We are not forgotten.

—*Carol Tokar Pavliska*

Miracle in Georgetown

He staggered in fifteen minutes after the traditional holiday hymn sing had begun, plopping with a thud into the wooden pew directly behind me. It was Christmas Eve night at historic St. Paul's Episcopal Church in the small and quaint town of Georgetown, Delaware, and midnight Mass was scheduled to commence in about twenty minutes. Dozens of candles cast a warm glow throughout the church. Accompanied by the pipe organist, the congregation joined the choir in a unified voice of celebration and joy.

I recall smelling the strong odor of alcohol right behind me. Trying to appear inconspicuous, I nonchalantly turned at an angle while I continued singing so I could glance at the whiskey-breathed intruder. A young man, perhaps age twenty-five, maybe younger, sat alone in the pew, a drunken smile plastered across his unshaven face. His hair was bushy and uncombed, his clothing unbefitting a reverent church service. I did not recognize the fellow and later would learn that nobody else knew him either, which is odd in Georgetown, a friendly place where everyone seems to know everybody else and their family trees.

I immediately realized that the man was confused, and not just with the Christmas Eve service, which for a first-time visitor can be somewhat perplexing. He was disoriented, in general. He stumbled aimlessly through the hymnal and a prayer book like a child leafing through coloring books at the doctor's office. He was obviously intoxicated and his behavior made me uncomfortable. Judging by the numerous nervous stares I observed, targeted in the young man's direction, some subtle and some not so subtle, others shared my opinion.

A good-natured parishioner named Bob left his family and his regularly appointed pew and joined the fellow, shaking his hand and introducing himself with a warm smile. Bob helped the man throughout the remainder of the hymn sing, assisting the delighted guy with locating the proper songs and directing him with basic liturgical functions, such as when to stand, sit, and kneel. With each song, the drunken stranger sang zealously louder and genuinely off key, although I suspect he felt he was performing as well as

Pavarotti. I found his butchering of the traditional holiday carols both disturbing and amusing at the same time. Though he couldn't sing a lick, he certainly was having fun.

The hymn sing-along ended and the service began with "O Come All Ye Faithful," as a procession of priests in robes and acolytes bearing torches entered from the back of the church. Someone in the procession waved a canister of incense around, preparing the sanctuary for worship and God's presence, but it made my eyes water and I sneezed. The service continued with prayer and Bible readings about the birth of the Savior, the infant Jesus. Good Samaritan Bob continued to befriend the man, who grinned with delight, and I, my heart softening, traded smiles with him.

Why was I at first angry that he'd come here tonight? I thought. *This is God's house, not mine, and all are welcomed in the house of the Lord.*

I wondered whether the young man was lonely or depressed on this holiday eve, and had first sought the comfort of liquor, drowning unknown sorrows, and had somehow journeyed by our church. Perhaps he'd heard the festive Christmas music outside the ancient brick walls. Maybe he'd seen the church aglow through the windows, holly wreaths hanging from the huge oaken doors, like one of those wonderful Thomas Kinkade landscape portraits, so inviting. Perhaps something deep within his heart had prompted him to go inside. Maybe he simply needed to be in the warm company of other human beings. I wondered who he was and where he'd come from. Did he have a family? Was he married? Did he have children?

The priest moved to the pulpit to begin his Christmas homily. The father had preached for only a few minutes when he abruptly stopped his sermon. I initially thought that he'd lost his place or was pausing for oratorical effect. But then I noticed him looking upon the congregation with a concerned frown rippling across his forehead. A low, curious murmur spread throughout the congregation. Everyone, including myself, looked to where the priest was gazing. About four pews back from the front, on the left side, Bill, an elderly man who faithfully attended every Sunday, had slumped over. Several members of the congregation had moved to his aid, thinking he had merely passed out. The situation, however, was far graver.

The service came to a complete halt as one parishioner sprinted to call 911. Several people laid Bill on his back in the pew and attempted to revive him. Although a medical doctor and several nurses were on hand that evening, the matter did not appear good. Bill was unconscious, had stopped breathing, and his pulse was weak. Even from across the center aisle in dim lighting I could see his flesh turning gray.

Stunned, most of us just sat or stood in our pews, paralyzed with fear and disbelief. A beloved member of our church community was dying before our eyes, and suddenly it no longer felt like Christmas Eve. I felt helpless, lost. Then a voice spoke out.

"Why don't we all get down on our knees and pray for the old guy," the voice bellowed from behind me. It was our visitor, his voice slurred but strong. "Maybe God can help him."

Like a slap in the face, many of us snapped out of our panicked stupor and silently knelt in agreement with the man's suggestion. As several people continued to tend to Bill, who was near death, the rest of the congregation prayed in honest, pleading whispers. I prayed harder and more sincerely than I ever had, my wet eyes tightly shut.

Moments later, I heard a commotion to my left. I opened my eyes just as I whispered "Amen" and was shocked to see Bill sitting up, his eyes open, the paleness in his face rapidly disappearing. Happy sobs could be heard throughout the church; our prayers had been gloriously answered! Despite numerous inquiries, Bill assured us that he was fine. When the paramedics arrived, racing down the center aisle with their equipment and stretcher, he refused to go to the hospital, insisting on staying for the conclusion of the

Christmas Eve Mass. And after everything settled down, the service was, in fact, finished without further incident.

After the closing benediction and song—a rousing "Joy to the World"—I turned to shake the young man's hand, but he was gone. He had apparently left during the Eucharist as the congregation filed pew by pew for the bread and wine, the body and blood of our Savior.

I later discovered that no one else had seen the man leave, either. It was as if he'd appeared out of nowhere and then simply vanished into thin air. No one knew his identity or anything about him. He was no one's relative or neighbor or coworker. No one knew or ever saw again the man who visited us that Christmas Eve, when a whole church witnessed a miracle. A dying man was revived, saved from death, by prayer initiated by a stranger, a person like you or me, or perhaps the guy we pass every day in the street and pay no attention to, an unlikely angel who prays for our health and happiness, for peace and goodwill to all.

—David Michael Smith

Christmas Bread Pudding

When I was a girl, the biggest present under the Christmas tree was always for my mother. Each year my father would go to one of the downtown department stores, find a salesclerk that reminded him of my mother, and ask for her help in choosing a gift. Several days before Christmas he would slip the present under the tree, where the store-wrapped box with its shiny paper and big bow stood out against the other, home-wrapped presents.

On Christmas morning my mother's present was the last one opened. It would be a new dress or suit, always much nicer than anything she would buy for herself. As soon as she opened the box, my father would start offering to return the present and buy something else. My mother repeatedly assured him the new clothes were exactly what she wanted.

I knew that, despite his anxious questions, my

father was pleased with his gift and that he loved my mother. I knew my mother worried that the present was too extravagant and returned his love. It was all part of the holiday tradition.

Later when my father started his own business, my parents agreed not to exchange presents at Christmas. I am sure my mother was the one who initiated this economy, since she managed the household expenses. She probably suggested putting their money toward some household repair or buying presents only for the children. But on Christmas morning a present for my mother always appeared from the trunk of my father's car. My mother, who had kept her part of the bargain, would exclaim, "You promised!"

This went on for years. My sisters and I encouraged our mother to buy our father a Christmas present.

"No," she would say, "This year we agreed not to do that."

But every year my father, the man who drilled into his daughters the importance of honoring the commitments we made, broke his promise and gave my mother a present. It became clear to me that a promise not to give presents was one that did not need to be honored.

My own approach to Christmas reflects the influence of both parents. Like my mother, I am a bit of a holiday curmudgeon. I worry about money. I complain when any evidence of Christmas is seen before the

Thanksgiving turkey is carved. I rail against the consumerism of crowded shopping malls, and my tolerance for Christmas music is exhausted long before December 25.

But like my father, I enjoy giving gifts. I appreciate that my attitudes are inconsistent. I already own more than I need, as do most of the people on my gift list, and I would prefer to pick out any significant purchase for myself. Still, simplicity is not what I want for Christmas.

What I want from the people I love is excess. From my husband, I want romantic declarations. From my family, I want unconditional acceptance. From my friends, I want to be remembered. In short, I want to sit down in front of my Christmas tree, drink a glass of good champagne, and open presents—not cards announcing gifts given in my name.

Last year it was decided that my parents, sisters, and I would draw names and be responsible for giving only one Christmas present. This was a sensible decision, acknowledging the differences in our lifestyles and financial obligations. Like many families these days, we don't see each other regularly and don't always know each others' tastes or interests. But my father and I disliked the idea, and we called each other weekly to complain.

"I don't see what the problem is," I said. "I like giving presents."

"So do I," my father sighed. "And frankly, I like getting them."

Christmas afternoon my father gave each of his daughters a piece of jewelry. I immediately put on my string of malachite beads and pulled out a cookbook for my father from my tote bag.

My middle sister, who has inherited a different mix of our parents' holiday traits, glared at us both and said, "You promised."

But what kind of promise is that? Why should I agree not to remember you so that you don't need to bother remembering me?

Recently I read a recipe for Christmas bread pudding in a Shaker cookbook that started me thinking about how I approach the holidays. The recipe called for:

> . . . [T]hick slices of bread generously buttered
> . . . a goodly layer of currants spread with straw-
> berry jam, not too thin, for remember it is
> Christmas! Pour over this an unboiled custard
> made of plenty of eggs and rich milk, for remember
> it is Christmas! Bake until the crust is well set and
> the top is a rich and appetizing golden brown. Eat
> it with much relish, for remember it is Christmas!

I am not fond of bread pudding. What attracted me to the recipe was the childlike enthusiasm I remember from those early Christmases when the biggest present under the tree was for my mother. In the confusion of our daily lives it is tempting to pare away our commitments until we are left with a solitary precious bauble. But even the Shakers with their love of simplicity knew that there was a time and a place for bread generously buttered and jam thickly spread. Holidays include glitter and excess. They are about accepting the uncertainty, the unfairness—and the gifts—of our lives. For remember, it is Christmas!

—*Karen Ackland*

Is That All There Is?

Sally's mother, Ethel, lived just down the block, and she knew that some family secrets were impossible to keep. Her son-in-law had a reputation in the neighborhood. A neighbor once asked Ethel about her daughter, Sally's, marriage and was told, "Our Pete, he's a nice guy when he's sober, but he's a drinker and a gambler."

"Pete took up gambling to reward himself the first time he got sober," Ethel explained. "Like all the drinkers I've ever known, Pete thought he was entitled to a substitute, a reward for not drinking. Of course, when he went back to drinking after a few months, he forgot to trade in the gambling. I don't know how Sally puts up with him."

People loved Pete because of his sober personality. He was a tall, outgoing fellow with a smile and a joke for everyone.

Sally's mother knew about drinkers because she'd married one herself and had stuck with him for years. "Pete never abused Sally," said the mother-in-law in feeble defense. "He leaves enough money every month for them to scrape by, and Sally has her job, too."

Those who knew him realized that Pete was a sentimental fellow, a bit of a dreamer. By the time Thanksgiving time came around every year, he was already imagining the whole script for Christmas. Every year he lectured the family on the coming joy of the season.

"This year is going to be different," he'd announce. "The tree will be glorious. It's going to have more lights, more tinsel, and more expensive ornaments than any of you can imagine. The whole living room, why, we'll stack it with beautiful presents, all wrapped in velvet ribbon and fancy paper. You'll see."

Pete was a salesman; he was just doing what came naturally.

Sally, as patient a wife as ever there was, never argued with Pete. Sometimes she tried to tell him the truth in a gentle way. When he talked about buying her a new car, she would smile and say, "Pete, I ride a bus to go clean other people's homes. I don't think that will change soon."

The children rolled their eyes and thought up excuses to leave the room when their dad starting dreaming about Christmas.

"Kids," said Pete as the children found reasons to leave, "this is going to be our greatest Christmas ever. We'll sing and eat and play together. . . ."

When Sally expressed doubt, Pete told her, "All it's going to take is a big win at the poker table down at the club. I see people leaving that game with bundles of cash all the time. It's my turn soon. I can feel it."

Year after year, of course, Pete gambled away first his pre-Christmas paycheck and then his yearly bonus, telling himself he was doing it for his family. He didn't understand that he wasn't gambling for money; he was gambling to get high just the way he did with alcohol.

Year after year, after leaving his money in the bars or at the card tables, he ended up swiping a scraggly tree or buying a broken leftover. He used what credit he could get to buy presents nobody seemed to want. The children's cheap toys broke the first day, and his wife's dime store perfume went unopened into a drawer with fifteen other unopened bottles.

"Pete, every year you wind up feeling sorry for yourself because your Christmas fantasy always turns to dust," his mother-in-law told him. "Then you think it's alright to get drunk on Christmas Day. Along about noon, you decide to teach those 'brats,' as you call your kids when you're drinking, a lesson. You get angry, you scream at the kids, and you finally toss their little tree into the yard. The neighbors ignore the whole mess, but I hear about it, Pete. Then Sally gets to take the children to spend Christmas night at her sister's house, and you, Pete, sit home alone feeling sorry for yourself. If Christmas came more than once a year your marriage would have been over long ago."

There seemed to be nothing anyone could ever do or say to fix things or change things or make it come out right.

Then one Christmas the kids were no longer kids. Pete and Sally's oldest son was seventeen, and Pete had no idea of what to buy an adolescent.

"Let's not talk about it right now," said his son when Pete started up with him about the coming Christmas.

"Look, son, I'm trying. You know that, and I won't kid you," said Pete. "In fact, I've been getting to a few Alcoholics Anonymous meetings, and the sober periods are getting longer. One of the guys with a gambling problem even took me to a Gamblers Anonymous meeting.

"Son," said Pete, "just tell me what would make you happy this year."

To Pete's credit, he was sober when he'd asked this question, and when he was sober he could be the loving father he was 90 percent of the time.

What the son said in answer to Pete's protest, to his question of what was wanted for Christmas, surprised the father.

The boy said, "I know you're trying, Dad, but please, you just forget Christmas. Let us do it all this year. We kids have jobs, so we have some money. Don't plan anything. Don't buy anything. You just forget Christmas. Let us do it all ourselves, and you be our guest. That's the only present we want from you."

There was no anger in the boy's voice, and Pete knew his son meant what he said.

Crazy, ungrateful kids, thought Pete. *Okay, I'll show them. Let them try to do it. They'll see how hard it is to plan a decent Christmas.*

Strangely enough, that Christmas just a little of the wisdom of the Alcoholics Anonymous program—something about giving up pride and self will—had penetrated Pete's thinking. He let the family write the script, and he even stayed sober, perhaps out of spite as much as love.

On Christmas Eve he sat quietly through dinner drinking only coffee, and then he watched as the children set up a small tree bought with their odd-jobs money. His wife helped them decorate the tree with paper chains and popcorn and cranberry strings that the kids made themselves. There were big red bows on the tree made with leftover ribbon from past years.

"Fine. Great work," said Sally, admiring the scene. "Now, children, let's get the presents."

They brought out their presents wrapped in plain

white paper and red ribbon. The son said, "There's just one little present for each of us from each person. We made them ourselves."

There were even presents with tags signed "Dad" for everyone. But, of course, being as he was only an actor in somebody else's script that year, Pete hadn't bought or wrapped a thing himself. The presents, in their simple wrappings, looked elegant under the tree.

They took turns reading, then, from "The Night Before Christmas." Even Pete took a turn and growled out a few of the famous lines. He was amazed when, out of the corner of his eye, he saw the kids all looking at him with tenderness. He hadn't seen them look so happy in years.

That evening they sang together, ate together, and played together, acting out a loving, if unfamiliar, script.

It was getting late on Christmas Eve, and being sober was beginning to bother Pete. "Is that it? Is that all there is?" he wanted to know.

"No, we're all going to midnight services together," said his wife, struggling with fear. Surely, she thought, this is the last straw; he's going to blow any minute.

Who can say why, but Pete did go with them to church, and the preacher said something that stuck in Pete's mind.

"Discipline," said the preacher, "is the path to

freedom. Only when we follow a few simple rules, what people call rituals, only then can we see the spiritual message upon which a celebration is based."

Pete, lost in thought, walked slightly behind the family as they returned from church. Everyone was admiring how the neighborhood looked in Christmas lights.

"How can it be," he wondered, speaking to no one in particular, "that doing what others want could give me what I've been searching for?"

On Christmas Day they opened the presents together. Then, Pete, instead of taking the first drink, went to an AA meeting and got home in time to attend services again with the family. What Pete finally realized is that doing less is often better.

He remembers coming home from church that first sober Christmas and, with a chuckle, asking the family once more, "Is that all there is?"

What they had done was so common, so ordinary, and it felt so good.

"Yes," his son said, "that's all. Wasn't that enough?"

The father had only tears for answer.

—*Julian Taber*

The Story of the Christmas Angel

Christmas at our house centers on the tree: majestic, bejeweled, bedecked, and artificial. Red poinsettia lights gleam among handcrafted ornaments. Here and there, specialty decorations hang proudly. There's the wooden football Paul made when he was seven. Toward the front is a tiny birdcage commemorating Rachel's dearly departed parakeet. Next to it is the stuffed snow baby that marked Tim's first Christmas. Every item on the tree is an artifact of our lives.

Holding court at the very top is our Christmas angel. She's strangely out of synch with the glitz and glitter of the rest of the decorations. She has a little doll face with yellow yarn hair. Her gown is avocado green burlap. Her wings are white felt stretched over wires. Although her eyes are closed, she's smiling as if she has a delightful secret she can't wait to share.

This year is different. The last of my children is grown, so I decide to retire our Christmas angel. In her place, I position a glorious golden figurine. She's also an angel, but with a white silk dress, a delicate porcelain face, and gossamer wings. She's a perfect fit for the top branch. She completes the tree.

Delighted with the results, I turn to see Tim, my youngest, looking at her. Twenty-one years ago, I brought him home in a Christmas stocking. Now he's six foot two, almost as tall as the tree. The lights reflect in his eyes.

I blink twice. . . .

Instead of Tim, I see five-year-old Timothy gazing up in wonder, straining to see the top of the tree.

"Mommy, Mommy," Timothy cried. "Tell the angel story, p-l-e-a-s-e."

Just then, Rachel swooped in, dressed as the angel Gabriel. Her white slip was the angel's gown; gold tinsel doubled as a halo. She flapped her towel wings, practicing for our family Christmas pageant.

"Oh, p-l-e-a-s-e, Mom, not that again." This from the angel Gabriel. "Every year we have to hear the same ole story about that stupid angel." She flapped her wings. "Give it a rest."

I decided to stay out of it and hung another ornament.

Timothy grabbed the end of Rachel's towel. "She's not stupid." He gave the towel a yank.

Rachel tugged back. "Is, too."

At that moment, my middle child, Paul, entered the melee. "Hey, look it, if we're going to do this, Timothy's got to put this on." He threw a bathrobe at his little brother.

"I'm not gonna be the baby Jesus again this year." Timothy crossed his arms, indignant.

"The youngest always plays baby Jesus. It's a tradition." Paul loved to direct.

"I'm too old to be baby Jesus!"

"See, that's what I mean about the Christmas angel story," Rachel said pointedly. "We're too old for it."

"I'll never be too old for it," our former baby Jesus said. "Mom, please tell it."

I gathered the three of them together near the tree. "First, Paul, why don't we use one of Rachel's dolls as baby Jesus this year."

Timothy let out a huge sigh of relief.

"And," I continued, "I'll tell the Christmas angel story as long as there is someone who wants to hear it."

I drew Timothy into my lap and began the story. I told about the first year that their dad and I were married. Lee was still in college and we lived in student housing. So it was no surprise that we couldn't afford anything for Christmas that year. No decorations, no presents. Then, on Christmas Eve, we saw a tree lot owner giving out the last of his trees for free.

First Paul and then Rachel drew nearer.

"And the only trees left were the ones no one wanted," Rachel supplied.

"Yes, the only trees left were small or broken, but we looked anyway. Way in the back, we found a three foot tree, straight and strong."

"But it had only five branches," prompted Paul.

"But you took it home anyway," Rachel added.

"Then what?" asked Timothy, although he already knew the answer.

"Dad and I put all of our change together and bought one ornament for the very top."

"The angel . . ." breathed Timothy.

"Yes, the angel."

We all looked to the top of the tree.

In unison, we said, "Every year since, the Christmas angel has been on the top of our tree."

She smiled down at us.

I blink twice. . . .

On top of the tree, I see a golden glorious angel with gossamer wings.

Tim looks down at me from his very adult height. "Where's the Christmas angel?"

"I thought this would be a good year to put her away." Strangely, there is a lump in my throat.

The front door bursts open, flooding the room with airport arrivals: Rachel and her husband, Rob, with their two children, Justin and Reagan. At the same time, Paul and his wife, Jami, arrive with their daughter, Cyrah.

The three grandchildren grab me around the knees. I almost fall over with all the kisses and hugs. Justin is eleven, and Cyrah just turned ten. This is three-year-old Reagan's first Christmas with us.

While everyone struggles with suitcases, taking them upstairs, Rachel gives me a quick embrace. Paul and Tim exchange some sort of masculine hand jive.

"Mom bought a new angel," Tim announces.

"What!" Rachel is incredulous. "Every year since," she quotes, "the Christmas angel has been on the top of our tree." She glares at me as if daring me to deny it. "It's a tradition."

"Oh, no, the angel story," Cyrah groans. She's Paul's daughter, all right, our drama queen. "Not that."

"Me want story." Reagan pulls me to sit down so I have a lap for her to crawl into. "Tell me, tell me!"

"You have to, Mom," Rachel says. "Remember, you said as long as there is someone who wants to hear the story."

Without further ado, Tim plucks the glorious angel with gossamer wings from the top of the tree. No need for prompting, Lee brings the wrapped bundle out of storage. Everyone draws around the tree. The tiny red lights sparkle against the ornaments. Jami and Paul gather Cyrah close to them.

Justin lays his head against Rachel's shoulder. Rob puts his arm around them.

I carefully unwrap our Christmas angel.

"Ohhh!" breathes Reagan, as the yellow yarn hair and avocado green angel robe are uncovered.

Everyone watches Lee position the angel in her old spot on the treetop. She smiles down at us as if she has a delightful secret she can't wait to share.

I draw Reagan into my lap and begin the story.

—Kristl Volk Franklin

Christmas Dinner, Christmas Spirit

Almost 4:30. Quitting time at Social Services. My coworkers were already gathering their coats and gloves and heading out to clear snow from their windshields so they could get home to finish last-minute shopping and spend Christmas Eve with their loved ones. I was sacking up the Christmas dinner I'd bought from the deli. With the hectic schedule of a single mother, a fast turkey dinner was better than none at all for my four-year-old son and me. I had wrapped presents for Joey in the trunk of my car and a brand-new Chipmunks Christmas CD and portable player for him in my purse. I was ready to rock out the Christmas vacation with Joey and the Chipmunks and spend some leisure time at home with my rambunctious boy.

Just then, at 4:30 on the dot, the phone rang. Everyone else had left, and I could have ignored it.

After all, it was quitting time, officially. And it was the start of Christmas vacation. So no one would have been the wiser had I just slinked out the back door and gone to my car.

But I'd have known, and it was the guilty pang that made me lift the receiver. We were Social Services, and it was probably an emergency.

"Hi, Tammy? This is the sheriff. We got a phone call from old Miss Mabel. She called and said she needed someone to drop off her prescription."

I groaned inwardly. *They call this an emergency? Don't they know we do investigations? Emergency-type things? And it's Christmas, for Pete's sake! I should be home dancing around the living room with my son to the Chipmunks. Eating that good turkey dinner and putting presents under the sparkly tree.*

Why can't you drop it off? I wanted to ask. *Or get a deputy to? Why do I have to do something that even one of her neighbors could do?*

It wasn't like Mabel's house was on my way home. She lived ten miles in the opposite direction. And it really wasn't my duty. I didn't have to do it. Delivering prescriptions to clients did not appear on our job descriptions.

But I found myself, for whatever nutty reason, saying, "Okay, I'll do it."

Grumbling, I hung up the phone, swung on my coat, picked up my turkey dinner, and left the office, locking up behind me.

After picking up the medication at the pharmacy, I proceeded up the two-lane country road to Miss Mabel's. The curvy road was downright treacherous with the wet snow covering it.

Mabel lived alone. Her family lived out of the area and rarely visited. She could be cranky and demanding. She had the police department and community services hopping to meet her every whim.

Well, I'd give her what for. *Didn't she realize we had lives, too? Families? Holidays?* My job already took so much time away from my son, Joey.

Her house was small and unkempt because she stubbornly insisted on doing her own household chores rather than letting Senior Services do them. She used a walker, and her balance was poor, yet she managed to bathe herself and cook and clean, in a marginal way.

As I pulled into her gravel driveway and carried her medicine to the front door, her house not only looked untidy, it seemed downright sad. No Christmas lights adorned her porch. No decorated tree blinked in her window. No wreath hung on her door.

"Miss Mabel!" I called as I knocked on the door. "I have your medicine!"

I waited for an answer. She was hard of hearing, so I raised my voice.

"Miss Mabel! I have your medicine!"

I heard her knocking around inside. Having been

acquainted with her for years, I knew she was getting her walker and making her way to the door.

Sometimes I wondered why she just didn't go to a rest home. I'd spoken to her several times about it. She would have companionship, supervision, round-the-clock health care, security. But she would have none of it. And since she was competent, she could choose to live where and how she wanted to. I sort of admired her spunk. I'm not so sure I'd want a social worker barging in and telling me where I needed to go.

"Terry!"

She always got my name wrong. Sometimes she called me Tabby, sometimes Tara, sometimes Tanya. But it was okay. I knew she recognized me.

"Thank you so much!" she cried as she took the medicine from me. "Won't you come in?"

"Oh, no, I can't. I need to get home. My son is waiting for me."

"Just for a minute" she said, reaching for my coat sleeve.

She practically dragged me inside, so I went.

"Do you have everything you need?" I asked her. "Gas in the tank? Water not frozen? Groceries?"

"Oh, I'm fine. The grocery boy brought my supplies today. Come on in and sit down."

"No, really. I should get going."

She smiled, and tears suddenly came to her eyes. "Your little boy, right?"

I nodded.

"I had a little boy. Who grew into a big boy. Who now lives in Canada."

I nodded. "George, right?"

"You remember!"

"Well . . ." I shrugged. She talked about him all the time. How could I forget?

I looked around her living room. So drab and unfestive. No Christmas cards, no Christmas cookies, no decorations, no candy canes.

"What are you doing for the holidays?" I asked. "Is George coming to see you?"

"He can't. He got laid off and can't afford to travel. He called me, though."

I nodded again. But this time I couldn't leave. Not like this. Not with her standing so alone in the middle of her living room.

"Do you have turkey?" I asked her.

"Why, no, I don't. Why?"

"Well . . ."

Gosh, I should be on my way home. I should be home with my little boy, handing him presents for the tree. We should be laughing to the silly Chipmunk songs. Or playing in the snow.

"How about we eat Christmas dinner together? I'll take you to my house and bring you back later this evening?"

"No, I don't want to go out. It's too cold. And I'm

afraid I might fall."

She had a point. And I could get in big-time trouble for taking a client to my home.

"How about I bring Christmas dinner to you then?"

"What do you mean?"

"I'll be right back."

She watched eagerly at the front door as I trekked through the mounting snow to my car.

Please, Joey. Forgive Mommy this one time for being late for the holidays. I'll make it up to you, I promise.

I packed in our Christmas dinner, figuring I could get more for Joey and me on my way home, a Christmas card, even the Chipmunks CD and portable player. Spying her big potted plant in the corner, I moved it in front of her window and draped it in Christmas lights.

"Tasha! How beautiful!"

We laughed and ate deli turkey, mashed potatoes, corn, rolls, and pie at her kitchen table. She talked about George, and I talked about Joey. I didn't do it to be a martyr; I did it because it felt like the right thing to do. There was no way I could have gone to sleep that night with the image of that forlorn old woman standing by herself in her Christmas-less house.

When I left, she kissed my cheek at the door.

"Thank you. Merry Christmas, Tammy."

—*Tammy Ruggles*

A Long Way from Anywhere

The seven-year-old girl sat quietly on the concrete steps of the old, gray apartment complex, waiting for her mommy and daddy to come down with the last few items that would fit into their dilapidated, old Ford. She wrapped her torn and stained blue blanket around her chubby shoulders and cuddled her handmade clown doll to her chest. Taking a deep breath, she blew out a resigned sigh and watched her warm breath turn to crystal as it touched the early-morning air.

Here we go again, she thought. *Another trip to who knows where.*

Her bright blue eyes grew dark as her parents hurried down the stairs with only a few items between them.

"Where is Mr. Fuzzy Teddy?" she asked.

Without a word, Mommy gently ushered the

little girl into the backseat of the car. The child sat with her arms crossed. She knew another toy was being left behind because there "wasn't room" for it. She had heard the line so many times she wondered why she still asked. The last time they'd moved, her favorite doll had been left behind. The time before that, it was her appaloosa rocking horse. The time before that, her four-foot-long, green stuffed snake with the rainbow-colored spots.

Each time something was left behind, if felt like a piece of her heart had been sliced off with a big sharp carving knife. Since she was an only child and had no friends, her toys were her companions. To lose them was heart wrenching, but she suffered in silence. If she said anything, Daddy would just feel bad and go even more quiet than normal. His cold shoulder was harder to take than the breaking of her heart.

As they drove away, a salty tear rolled down her plump, pink cheek as she watched the red and green lights flash by her window. It was Christmas Eve, and they were on the road again. She really thought that this year they were going to have a "real" Christmas. Mommy and she had put up a tiny, scrawny tree they'd found out in the field. She had helped decorate it with popcorn and paper stars. They had even placed a teeny straw baby Jesus on one of the branches.

Now, they were driving away from the promise of Christmas. She wasn't sure where they were going, only that they were heading in the direction of California. They always headed to California when the money was running out. Daddy had a sister there who always let him "borrow" money and let them stay with her a few days until Daddy could "get back on his feet."

As the blustery day wore on, the little girl played in the backseat with her blanket, handmade clown doll, and a bright green plastic jump rope with missing handles. Sitting on the edge of the Ford's tattered bench seat, she'd drop the rope down a rust hole in the floor right beneath her feet. With a little help from her fingers, she had made the hole big enough so that she could watch the rope dance and jerk as its end hit the road flashing by. It kept her quiet for hours.

As day rolled into stormy night, her stomach tied into a tighter and tighter knot. Christmas would be there in no time, and they had no tree, no fireplace, and no place to stay so Santa could find her. Yet, she remained silent. Words were of no help when Daddy was involved.

As night fell, they pulled into a small, well-used truck stop diner for dinner. They ordered two of the "specials," which, in honor of the holiday, consisted of sliced turkey, dressing, and mashed potatoes and gravy. Everything tasted so good to her. She even got to share a piece of pumpkin pie with Mommy and Daddy. Maybe Christmas Eve on the road wasn't so bad after all. At least they were together.

It was late by the time they'd finished dinner, washed up in the bathroom, and hit the road again. The tired child lay down on the backseat, curled up under her thin blue blanket, and imagined the Christmas they would have next year. She pictured a big home with enough rooms so that everyone had their own special place. She saw a big Christmas tree sparkling with hundreds of green, yellow, red, and blue lights. Silver tinsel hung from every branch. Popcorn and paper chains encircled its limbs. Under the tree sat dozens of brightly colored packages, many of them with her name on them. In her mind she opened the biggest package and out popped a three-foot panda bear. She fell asleep with a smile on her face and a tear on her cheek.

Morning seemed to come early, and they were still driving. When she woke up, she felt the chill of the icy outside air as it poured in from the hole in the floor and the leaky windows. She wrapped the blanket closer around her shoulders, sat up, and crossed her legs under her to keep her feet warm. After yawning and wiping the sleep from her eyes, she turned to look out the window.

There by her side lay a little, bald baby doll wrapped in a pink blanket, a brand-new Mickey Mouse coloring book, and a fresh box of eight Crayola crayons. She picked up the toys without a word and just stared at them for a while.

"Mommy," she finally said in a whisper.

"Yes," her mom whispered back.

"Where did these toys come from?"

"Santa brought them," she said.

"But how?"

"Santa always finds good little girls and boys, even when they're a long way from anywhere."

The little girl sat back in the seat and played quietly for hours with her new toys.

That little girl was me, and I found out many years later that my mom and dad had stopped at a convenience store and used their last two dollars to purchase those toys. What should have been the worst Christmas of my life turned out to be the best Christmas, because my parents gave me more than toys. They gave me a belief in miracles.

—*Candace Carteen*

Figure of Love

Each summer at our annual family gathering, the ritual signaling the end of the reunion is the Christmas gift-exchange draw. The family members who are present draw names from a hat, and those who are absent draw a name by proxy with Mother's help. This ensures that we have plenty of time to buy the perfect Christmas gift for our recipient.

The Christmas draw has been a matter of many discussions over the years, as the members of our family don't all enjoy the same level of income. The younger children and even newlyweds are at a distinct financial disadvantage when it comes to being able to purchase a gift that doesn't pale in comparison to one offered by a well-to-do sibling. For this reason, we have set a price limit on how much each person can spend on the gift. This year someone suggested that we raise the price limit.

As we cleared away the dishes from our final meal together, I entered the kitchen to find my mother gazing wistfully at a small rubber figurine. Old and cracked, this figure has sat on the windowsill above her sink for more than thirty years. It is a childish thing and I've often wondered why she keeps it there. Fashioned from pink and blue molded rubber, the figure depicts a young boy, his baseball cap askew and a rubber bat half hidden behind his back. Perhaps it was the look on her face or maybe it was the discussion we had just had about Christmas gifts, but suddenly a flood of memories washed over me, and I finally understood why the rubber figure has remained over her sink all these years.

I'm eight years older than my brother, and at the sophisticated age of thirteen, I'd felt I had a pretty good idea of what did and did not constitute an appropriate Christmas present for our mother. Five-year-old boys, on the other hand, didn't have a clue as to how to buy a decent gift. So, with our hard-earned savings stuffed deep into our pockets, my brother and I set out together on a shopping expedition to buy what I was sure would be two perfect Christmas presents for Mom. After carefully considering many price tags, I finally settled on a gift that relieved me of my entire savings. My brother, on the other hand, hadn't been happy with anything he saw.

As luck would have it, on our way home we were forced to wait at a bus stop located in front of a secondhand store, and there in the window he spotted the perfect gift for Mom. No amount of pressure on my part could dissuade him from buying the small rubber figure of a little boy holding a baseball bat. His reasoning was that Mom liked to watch him play ball and she liked the color blue. He knew she'd love it. I, on the other hand, was mortified that he would spend only twenty-five cents on our mother's Christmas present.

On Christmas morning he was flushed with pride as he handed her his gift. Eyes shining, he watched every movement of her hands as she carefully unwrapped the crumpled layers of paper that covered the rubber figure. As the paper fell away, he could no longer contain his excitement and he leaped and twirled in front of her, crying, "Isn't it great!" I didn't understand how Mom could be so happy getting such a goofy gift, and I was surprised when she'd placed it on the windowsill above the sink.

I no longer remember what I bought my mother that Christmas, and I'm sure she doesn't remember, either. What I do remember is that I'd chosen my gift for its dollar value, thinking the price tag made it a proper present.

My brother, on the other hand, in his childish innocence, had given no thought to the price. He had given for the joy of giving, and his joy had multiplied the value of the gift. My mother's present that Christmas had not been a little rubber figure; it was the gift of her son's love, his excitement and enthusiasm for life, captured in a plastic statue of a happy little boy much like her own.

A series of bad choices has made my brother's life a hard one, and we rarely see him at family functions. I'm sure the little figurine on the windowsill is kept there as a reminder of a time when my mother's child received, and gave, such joy from a gift whose value cannot be measured in dollars, only in love.

—*Rita Y. Toews*

Christmas Angels

Dad began celebrating the holiday early and hadn't been home for two days. Anticipating his return, little Maggie ran to the window every time she heard a noise outside.

"Daddy's home with our Christmas tree! I knew he'd keep his promise."

Though we sisters had walked a long trail of broken promises with him, Maggie still had unwavering faith in his word, and she fiercely defended him.

"That wasn't him, but he's coming any minute."

Ahnna scraped a small circle of ice from the window with a razorblade so Maggie could continue to watch for him. Pressing her face against the glass, her warm breath made it foggy, and she wiped it each time with a wad of toilet paper.

An oil-burning heating stove stood in a corner of the living room, and we often lay on the thin carpet in front of it watching the flames dance on the other side of its isinglass window. Frigid winds carried heavy wet snow across Lake Erie from Canada, forcing the little stove to run constantly.

Mama lay on the couch huddled under a feather-tic blanket. She had promised all week that we would bake cookies today, but it was almost noon and she showed no sign of getting up. Approaching her timidly, Ahnna and I were afraid to speak and stood mutely staring at her.

"What are you two staring at? What do you want?" Mama sounded angry, and we didn't want to make her mad.

Maggie left her place at the window and joined us, exclaiming, "We want to bake the Christmas cookies, Mama. C'mon. Get up so we can start. Daddy will be here soon with our tree and then we'll get too busy."

Ahnna quickly added, "You promised, and we've been waiting all day."

Scowling at us, she blurted, "I can't get up. I'm sick. Cookies aren't so important, are they? Do you want me to get sicker, just so you can have cookies?"

She didn't look sick. Her cheeks were pink, and her eyes were sharp and clear with no tears. Earlier she had gone to the bathroom and come out with her hair combed and lips rosy with fresh lipstick.

Stepping forward, I said, "Mama, you don't look sick. You really don't."

Ahnna agreed and reassuringly said, "Mama, Catherine's right. We don't want you to get sick from making cookies, but you look fine. Can't you get up for just a little while? You can sit on a chair and tell us what to do. We'll do all the work."

Mama was adamant. "I said I'm sick. You don't know anything. You're just three dumb little girls. No! I can't get up, not even for a little while."

Immediately responding with guilt for being so selfish, we barraged her with questions. "Should we phone a neighbor? Should we call the doctor? What can we do to help you?" Maggie was crying as she squeezed onto the couch and tried to hug Mama.

"No! Don't do anything. I can take care of myself." Pushing Maggie away so hard that she tumbled to the floor, Mama then sat up and faced us. "You might as well know. There will be no celebration here. Daddy went drinking and didn't give me any money for Christmas. Now go away and stop pestering me."

Not wanting to believe what she said, we stood like rocks as she lay back and pulled the feather-tic over her head.

Maggie went back to her lookout at the window, while Ahnna and I retreated to the kitchen. Sitting quietly at the table, we were each lost in our own misery. My mind was racing as horrible thoughts swirled and crashed into each other. *No Christmas?*

No cookies? There's just got to be a celebration for Jesus'
birthday. No presents for Maggie? I don't believe it.
Mama's playing a trick on us. She has to be joking.

Maggie's excited hollering snapped me out of my
scary thoughts. "Daddy's home! I hear him! I hear
him!"

Swinging the door wide open, Maggie's hopes
dimmed when the mailman met her.

"Merry Christmas, little girl. It's a good thing
Santa and his reindeer fly through the sky. He'd have
a rough time with all this snow if he had to travel in
a car."

Taking the mail, Maggie blurted, "My daddy's
getting our tree and he's on his way home now."

One of the envelopes was for Ahnna. Tearing it
open, a five-dollar bill tumbled to the floor. It was a
handwritten card from her godmother, Aunt
Stephanie.

> *Dear Ahnna,*
> *Wishing you a wonderful Christmas. Use this*
> *to get something special for yourself.*
> *Love,*
> *Aunt Stephanie*

Though Maggie kept her vigil, by five o'clock
Daddy still hadn't arrived.

"It's okay," she announced. "Santa will bring our

tree when he comes with our presents."

Her unbounded, but childish, determination tore at our hearts, and Ahnna and I could only stare sadly at each other. We had learned years earlier that there was no Santa, but Maggie was only four years old and still believed.

Suddenly inspired, Ahnna stood up, grabbed my hand, pulled me into our bedroom, and spoke in a hushed whisper.

"Maggie will have Christmas. I have all that money from Aunt Stephanie. The drugstore is still open and maybe we can find a tree, too. C'mon, let's get Maggie to sleep. Don't tell Mama what we're doing."

I swore not to say a word, "Cross my heart and hope to die, I swear."

Quickly getting Maggie into her pajamas, we lay down on either side of our little sister and pretended to sleep. She wanted to talk about Santa, but we faked being tired and insisted she close her eyes. Soon we could hear her easy rhythmic breathing and knew she was asleep. Slipping off the bed, we silently left the room and put on our coats and scarves.

Anxious to avoid an emotional collision with Mama, we rushed through the living room to the front door. Ahnna stopped briefly and turned to her.

"Mama, we're going to the corner store. Maggie's asleep. We'll be right back."

Coming out of a sleepy stupor, Mama jeered,

"That money burning a hole in your pocket, Ahnna? Going to spend it all on candy? You're just like your father."

We exited fast before she could stop us.

It was still snowing and very dark, but the harsh winds had subsided. Shoving our hands deep into our pockets for warmth, we hurried along while Ahnna shared her thoughts.

"We'll get Maggie a baby doll that says 'Mama.' Do you think she'd like that?"

In my mind's eye I could see the pleasant image of Maggie hugging and rocking her doll. "Oh, yes, Maggie would love a baby doll."

Despite the cold, we were determined in our quest. To avoid the unshoveled sidewalks, we tramped into the street and followed tire tracks. After going three blocks we climbed over a snow-bank to follow a narrow footpath that led the way up a steep hill. Trudging through the fresh, deep snow, we arrived out of breath at the little plaza.

Stomping snow from my shoes and shivering from the cold, I chattered, "We were in such a hurry to leave, I forgot to put fresh cardboard over the holes in my shoes."

Ahnna groaned. "My socks are soaking wet, and my feet are freezing, too, but we can warm up in the store. C'mon, let's run. Last one there's a monkey's uncle!"

Laughing, we ran together and arrived just as the manager was locking the door.

Most of the lights were turned off and we could see a helper inside putting on her coat. We pounded frantically at the door until the manager opened it a crack and scolded us.

"We're closed. What are you doing out on such a night? Don't you know it's Christmas Eve? Go home."

Desperate words tumbled from both of us, telling him of our plight. Ahnna showed him the money to prove we weren't lying, while we continued to beg him to allow us inside. By then the helper had come close, and we wildly tried to convince her to help. Both stood silent and stared at us. Suddenly flashing a broad smile, the manager flung open the door.

"Okay, okay. Come in. But you must hurry so we all can get home to our families."

The helper took a shopping basket and followed as the manager helped us select Maggie's baby doll, cologne for Daddy, and perfume for Mama.

When we expressed concern about not having enough money to pay for so much, the manager told Ahnna, "Of course you have enough money. You have more than enough."

When she didn't think I saw her, Ahnna pointed at me and whispered, "My sister, Catherine, too."

I discreetly did the same for her.

Grinning and sending the manager a wink, the

helper hurried off to the checkout counter, where she secretly wrapped everything in gay holiday paper. Meanwhile, the manager whisked us aside, saying he wanted to show us the store tree.

Sitting on the table was a baby tree decorated with little candy canes, colorful balls, and silver strands of tinsel. Perched on top was a beautiful smiling angel with outstretched arms.

The tree was awesome, and we told the manager it was the prettiest tree we ever saw.

"Is your Christmas tree up already?" he asked. "I bet yours is beautiful, too."

Avoiding his eyes, we shuffled uncomfortably. Then, speaking at the same time, we said, "Oh, yes, ours is beautiful," and "No. We're not having a tree this year."

Ahnna was embarrassed and shot me a look that said, *Don't tell him.* But the cat was already out of the bag.

Watching us closely, the manager said, "Would you girls do me a big favor? We have so many decorations in the store taking up too much space, and we need to make room. Do you think you could manage to take this tree home with you?"

His question stunned us, but we recovered fast. Wildly excited, Ahnna spoke for both of us. "Yes, yes! We'll take the tree. Maggie will love it. We love it. Thank you, thank you so much!"

When we'd finished putting all the tree decorations into a paper bag, the helper called us to get our gifts.

"The total comes to four dollars and fifty cents. Here's your change." Pushing a fifty-cent piece into Ahnna's hand, they ushered us to the door. We hugged and said goodbye amid shouts of "Merry Christmas" and left the store with our precious cargo.

Ahnna carefully carried the bags of decorations and gifts, while I clutched the tree to my chest, not allowing it to touch the ground. Oblivious to the cold and our wet feet, light as feathers we eagerly approached home and Maggie.

"I can't believe what happened, Catherine," Ahnna exclaimed. "Mama always tells us to watch out for people, but she's never met anyone like them."

Stopping abruptly, she turned to me and whispered, "Catherine, maybe they weren't people at all."

Confused, I responded, "What are you saying, Ahnna? Of course they were people."

Tilting her head back and turning her blue eyes toward the heavens, she softy answered, "They weren't people. They were angels."

—*Patricia Lugo*

Ho Ho Hold On!

I won't do it this year. I'll not get myself worked up in a tizzy all in the name of providing a memorable Christmas for my family. I'll keep the gifts under control, and I'll keep a lid on all the trimmings and menus and parties and everything else that lands me in bed with the flu every year by New Year's Eve.

I can't even believe it's me who is saying these things. What happened to that bright-eyed young woman whose heart was lighter than the meringue snow clouds she made every year? What happened to her endless energy and abounding joy at anything that squeaked of Christmas? Am I not the one who always has a festive new outfit for every party, a sprig of mistletoe for every doorway, and a small, yet thoughtfully wrapped, gift for every mail carrier, hairstylist, and anonymous newspaper flinger or, for that matter, anyone who'd been just plain nice to me that year?

I'll tell you what happened.

I became a mom. And now I'm the one who's declaring a truce with the Domestic Christmas Faeries who haunt my tortured attempts at sleep each night. They win. I won't even play along this year. And my family will end up happier for it, of that I'm quite sure.

One moment stands out to me as the perfect example of my having gone a tad too far with the holiday bit. It was last year. I'd bundled up my four-year-old son and eighteen-month-old daughter in their fluffy winter coats, hats, and mittens. The air was brisk (okay, frigid), but still I dragged them out to the middle of a large courtyard with a giant, beautifully decorated pine tree.

Why, what a perfect setting in which to snap our holiday photo! my Christmas muse whispered in my ear.

Naturally, my kids chaffed at the notion of standing out in the wind next to a huge prickly thing, let alone of holding each other's hand and smiling. So what did I do?

"DO YOU HEAR ME? I SAID . . . 'SMILE'!"

The dude from *Full Metal Jacket* couldn't have delivered the line any better. Needless to say, last year's Christmas card was not a keepsake of Rockwellian proportions.

So now a different voice is buzzing in my ear. . . .

I do not need to make star-shaped croutons.

I do not need to make star-shaped croutons.
I do not need to make star-shaped croutons.

Nor does anyone really expect me to jam a bunch of cloves in pomegranates and place them in freshly polished silver bowls throughout the house. Every bedroom does not need its own Christmas tree, every pillow does not need a cinnamon potpourri sachet beneath it, and my husband's lukewarm reception to his flannel jammies won't change even if they come wrapped in a tower of antique hat boxes.

As the season is just beginning, I'm forcing myself to remember how it feels to wait until the kids are asleep before I begin the pleasure of wrapping presents—when it's pitch-black outside and I'm hunchbacked over the bed in the guest room trying to curl the perfect ribbon. By that time of day, no mother should be allowed near sharp objects, let alone be twirling the blades of dull hair-cutting scissors around like a war-weary samurai.

These are the reality checks that I am calling upon to help keep myself under control this year.

If I can't snap the perfect family photo, people will understand. Especially the hundred-some strangers I choose to keep on my card list, even though I haven't spoken with them since sending last year's "perfect" (not!) family photo. Come to think of it, maybe it's time to cut the cord with my high school piano teacher. And will my high school boyfriend's mother really notice how cute my kids are and call him in California to tell him? Will that idiotic former boss of mine look into my kids' eyes and realize, *So, that's why she took two maternity leaves in three years?*

All I ever really wanted to do was create the kind of memorable experiences I'd had as a kid. Pure magic. Hot cocoa and angels in the snow. A drive on Christmas Eve to look for Santa's sleigh in the sky. Music and love and cookies.

Cookies. I guess I can handle a batch or two of cookies. Santas and reindeer. Elves and angels. Holly leaves with little Red Hots that look like berries. Oh, good idea! . . . The Red Hots can double as the nose for Rudolph. And, if I steady my hand just right, I can probably pull off a little icing mustache to distinguish the gingerbread man from the gingerbread woman. They'll need a house, too, with little peppermint wheels for windows. And a Christmas tree with tiny Milky Way presents. Hey. Wait a minute . . . cinnamon sticks would make the perfect woodpile, dusted with confectioner's sugar for snow, of course.

Oh, what the hell.

Happy Holidays to everyone, in whatever level of participation you can muster. I've always felt that New Year's Eve is better spent on the couch anyway. Since I've become a mom, that is.

—*Julie Clark Robinson*

Daddy's Red Sweater

My any years ago, my mother gave my father a red V-neck sweater for Christmas. He looked so handsome in it with his black hair and dark brown eyes, that I, almost sixteen years old, thought he had to be the most wonderful person on earth and I was so proud he was my father.

I was the oldest child and used to ask to borrow his red sweater. It looked good with my black-and-gray skirt. Daddy never said no.

Mom used to wear it sometimes, too, especially when she was standing over the floor furnace eating ice cream in the middle of the winter.

As my sisters and brothers grew up, the sweater became one of their favorite things to borrow as well. Please understand, we let Daddy wear his sweater whenever he wanted to, but I don't remember any of us ever having to take it off for that reason.

Eventually, Daddy's red sweater settled in the hands of my youngest brother, Andy. He took it to college and kept it as an adult. As all five of us kids went about the business of our adult lives, the red sweater became a memory of our youth, a source of laughter and story swapping at family gatherings.

Buying Christmas presents for Daddy was a difficult task, as it is for many fathers. But the Christmas of 1989, with Daddy increasingly incapacitated and introspective due to a series of disabling strokes, Andy had a dilemma: What do you give a homebound senior citizen who chooses to live modestly?

The answer came like a revelation. On Christmas morning, packaged neatly in the finest holiday wrappings, Daddy received his red sweater as a Christmas present for the second time—twenty-one years after he'd first received it from our mother.

When Daddy died in August 1991, my stepmother asked if there was anything of his I wanted.

"Oh, yes. Please may I have Daddy's red sweater?"

I could not bear to think of losing that family treasure. It was given to me graciously.

I knew that I could not be selfish and keep the sweater all for myself, although I have to admit that I considered it. Frankly, I wondered why no one else thought to ask for the sweater. And I wondered whether it might have meant more to me than to the rest of my brothers and sisters.

That year as a gift for my sister, Joanne, I put the sweater in a Christmas box with a tag on it that said, "To Joey—From Daddy." Inside the box was a card with a message to keep it for a year, and then pass it on the next year to the next in birth order, Ray. Ray passed it on to Jean, and then Jean passed it on to Andy, the youngest. He had been three days shy of one year old the year Mom had given the sweater to Dad for Christmas.

Andy had to keep the sweater for two years, because I was unable to come home the following year for Christmas. When I got the box and the sweater back, I had to do something new. I put the sweater in an old Diamond department store box with my credit card from the Diamond inside. The Diamond had been closed for several years and it held fond memories for all of us. I added a poem and told Joey that she needed to add another special memory to the box. She had no trouble deciding what to add: a picture of Daddy wearing the red sweater, holding her two babies.

As the holiday crept nearer, Joey and I discussed what we were going to do for Christmas. Of course, the red sweater was the topic of conversation.

"I wonder why we never bought our own red sweaters," I said. Both of our eyes lit up like cartoon characters with light bulbs over their heads.

"Red sweaters for Christmas!" we said in unison.

Then, she said, "We never bought our own because we never needed one. We could always borrow Daddy's."

We needed six identical red sweaters.

I called her at work. "I found two and bought them. I think I can go to the other stores, if you think I should."

"Do it," she said.

It took two more trips, but I had six identical red sweaters.

I was so excited that I could hardly wait for the six of us to get together and for the others to open their sweaters.

Joey gave Ray the box that Daddy's sweater was in. He opened it and said, "I just might have to wear this sometime this year."

"I don't think so." Joey handed out the packages to everyone to open.

Jean started to cry. Andy laughed with joy. Ray chuckled and said, "I was just wondering if I could find six red sweaters for everyone for next year!"

Mom said, "You got me one, too!"

"Well, Mom, you have to have one, since you started it," one of us reminded her.

Joey made arrangements to have our pictures taken together in the portrait studio where she worked part-time. The day after Christmas, we all met at the mall for portraits. There were two group pictures, and singles of all of us, and some grouped with Daddy's sweater. They all were very good.

Then, Joey had another idea. "Let's get Mom a framed large one for her birthday."

We all agreed to keep it a secret for a month, which isn't an easy thing to do in this family, and to give it to her for her seventy-eighth birthday on January 25.

Mom had to pick her chin up off the floor when she saw the group portrait. It was beautiful. We hung it over the sofa in her living room.

Jean's daughter, Malinda, helped Ray hang the picture. "Okay, now all of you get behind the sofa and take a picture of everyone with the picture," she suggested.

"Good idea!" everyone said at once, while we pulled out the sofa and stood in our "correct positions" to have another picture taken.

The new red sweaters that each of us now owns have already been shared with others. Ray's wife has worn his; Joey's boyfriend has worn hers. My daughters want to know when they get to share Dad's original sweater.

My father has been gone ten years now, but his love and memory join us together each year at Christmas. Daddy's red sweater has become a living symbol of a hardworking, generous father who taught us the joy of sharing and family.

—*Lynn R. Hartz*

Christmas Cards
from Winston

I have a "junk" drawer in my office; within it are many treasures of no apparent value. There is a garlic press my mother-in-law bequeathed to me when her mother died, corks from the most delicious wines I've ever tasted, and scores of used erasers that come home from school with my kids every year in June, used, but still keepers. Worth saving, too, are the Christmas cards I receive every year from a "boy" named Winston.

I met Winston forty years ago, when he moved in next door to my childhood home. Each year, his Christmas card goes into my junk drawer. I just can't bear to throw it away.

In last year's card, Winston quoted a Nietzsche axiom that he'd lifted from *Conan the Barbarian*: "That which does not kill us, makes us stronger." He was referring, I believe, to my life with three growing sons. Winston lives alone, or with a lady love, I'm not sure which, but I know he has no children. He has often referred to how different our lives are: mine, that of a married mother of three living in an urban New Jersey town not far from Manhattan, his in a tiny village somewhere in New Hampshire, where a street address is not even needed and one must drive for many miles to get so much as a slice of pizza.

I cherish Winston's Christmas cards. The holidays give us a reason to reconnect with people we value. And his cards remind me of how wondrous my life looks to someone whose path has diverged greatly from mine. Likewise, his holiday greetings give me a glimpse into the blessings of Winston's life and into a fascinating world I might not otherwise know. I've never been to visit him in New Hampshire and probably never will, but I imagine him walking down a rose-lined lane to his mailbox, sitting in a garden of black-eyed Susans, or building (for he is a carpenter), or studying (for he is an academic), or quietly enjoying nature. I am intrigued by his quiet, solitary life among the wildflowers, just as he is fascinated by my life with my colorful, cacophonous family. Yet, there is no envy between us. We rejoice in one another's happiness.

Without Christmas cards, we would not connect in this way. We've tried e-mail, but for two kids who met in the fifties, its joy was fleeting. Phone conversations would be awkward, too. After all, I am married, and even though I was in fourth grade when my crush on Winston was sparked, my husband would be wary if I were to call Winston regularly.

But Christmas cards, and the letters we tuck in with them, seem to be just the right way of "catching up" during the season of sharing. Because we write only once a year, we don't expect the connection to change our day-to-day lives, though it most certainly enriches our inner lives. What we do expect of one another in that one card a year is honesty. We speak of our triumphs and milestones, as well as our tragedies, for example, when Winston lost his brother and I lost my mother. We relay new discoveries about life and love and ourselves, made during the passing year. With paper and ink, we explore the big questions: *Did I make a mistake? What do I fear? What do I want? Do I feel satisfied, or discontented? Am I really happy?*

When I met Winston he was a boy of ten. He wrote me letters in code, in pale, lemon juice ink that could be detected only by lighting a candle underneath the thin, white paper. We sailed paper airplanes into the flowering dogwood trees that lined our properties with notes on their wings: "When will you be home from school?" "Do you like me?"

In the many years since those days of innocence, we have learned to abandon code and, in the spirit of

Christmas and friendship, to commit our thoughts and truths to paper with candor and trust. No mere holiday greetings of cheer for us. We delve deeper, sharing what has transpired during the year and in our hearts, whether happy or sad. And the under-lying message—that we still care, after all these years, about one another, about each other's hopes and dreams and accomplishments—never changes.

Christmas, to me, means many wonderful things. Among the most wondrous is my yearly card from Winston. The card will eventually go into my junk drawer, his message filed forever in my heart.

—*Kathryn E. Livingston*

# The Purfect Tree

As I stood at the window of our Wisconsin Rapids farmhouse, watching the shower of snowflakes add another foot of white to the country-side, I worried.

How were we going to get through the heavy snow to chop down our Christmas tree?

Traditionally, two days before Christmas my brothers, sister, and I would ride in the horse-drawn sleigh over the river and into our woods to select the perfect fir tree. But that year, with only three days left before Christmas and the snow in the field already four feet deep, all thirteen of us children were feeling anxious.

"Dad, can't we take the horses and go cut our tree today?" I asked.

Dad looked up from cleaning his fingernails with his pocketknife and said, "We can't chance Nick and

Betsy gettin trapped in the snowdrifts. We'll just have to wait until the roads are passable and go into town and fetch a tree."

"But what if the horses can't get us into town, either?" my sister, Donna, asked. It was a plausible question, considering we lived five miles to our nearest neighbors in one direction and five miles to the nearest store in the other.

"Then I guess we won't have a tree this year," Dad said. "After all, when it comes to runnin a farm, there's more important things that need a'worryin about and a'tendin to than a Christmas tree."

"No tree?" we kids moaned in unison.

"Children," Mother scolded. "Go play. Your father has enough on his mind without you adding to it."

The next morning before the rooster's crow I was out of bed to see whether the snow had stopped. It hadn't. We were even more snowbound than the day before. In fact, the blare from the morning radio announced that the storm would worsen by nightfall, bringing high winds and a possible ice storm.

Gloom filled my ten-year-old heart. Now it was definite: We would not have a tree for Christmas.

That night after getting ready for bed and turning out the lights, I felt compelled to go to my bedroom window, kneel, and lift my voice to heaven in prayer. In the silence of my room, between a heart full of spilled tears that I wiped from my eyes and nose with the sleeve of my nightgown, I reasoned with God.

"God, please! If you send us a tree for Christmas—and it doesn't have to be perfect—I won't ask for any more store-bought presents, I promise."

As I opened my mouth to conclude my prayer using the appropriate ending, I heard the sound of a dozen voices saying "A-a-a-a-men!"

Startled, I opened my eyes and swung around. Scattered throughout the shadows of my bedroom were all my brothers and sisters, including the older ones, all on their knees, their hands clasped in prayer.

The following morning, Christmas Eve, I awoke to the scratchy static of the radio and the clatter of glass bowls being put on the table for our oatmeal. I scrambled from my bed and dashed to the window.

There, miraculously, standing in the snow, was a beautifully shaped tree just waiting to be decorated.

"Mom, Dad!" I yelled as I rushed downstairs and into the kitchen. "Look out the front room window. God gave us a tree for Christmas."

Throwing me an unbelieving look, Dad got up from the table, ambled over to the window, and said, "Well, I'll be darned. She's right. It seems the top of that old forty-foot pine snapped off during the storm last night and presented us with the *purfect* tree."

—Sylvia Bright-Green

Lessons from
an Ugly Shirt

As clothes went, it was kind of ugly: a blue denim, Western-cut shirt with purple pearl buttons. Polite people would stop at calling it gaudy. But to a couple of new high school graduates testing their first semester in college, it was the height of comfort and style. The epitome of cool in a jeans and T-shirt world.

The shirt belonged to my college roommate, David. And because I gave him free use of my stereo, he let me wear the shirt. Sometimes. When he wasn't wearing it. And since we knew the shirt had the power to drive college women wild (*Note:* we were a couple of hormone-crazed college guys who talked a better game than we actually played), it was hard to turn such power over to anyone else. Even to the guy who owned it.

But we shared the shirt, and as the semester

progressed, we shared our stories. David was in school by virtue of scholarships and grants. He was smart. That was obvious from our first meeting. He liked great music (Charlie Daniels and Asleep at the Wheel), good movies (*Smokey and the Bandit*), great literature (Harlan Ellison and Doc Savage pulp novels), and he knew the plot to every Bugs Bunny cartoon ever made. He also understood things like calculus and geometry and could read French when the occasion presented itself.

He worked hard to keep his scholarships, because without even one of them, he would be out of school and back on the farm. He always felt one transcript away from having to go home. And in David's home, there was always just enough money to make ends meet. His father died when he was twelve, and his mother worked as a nurse. She made enough to keep the family farm running, but there were few extras.

Sometimes David talked about his father, about his kind ways and his easy laugh. Usually it was late at night, on the way back from a meal at my folks' house or in the dorm just before bed, and the conversation always ended with tears that flowed from a river of memories and longings. Memories of a father ravaged by cancer at a time when his son was just coming into his own. Longings for opportunities missed, because disease does not understand about the bond between father and son. Nor does it care.

On the day before he left for college, his mother took him to his favorite restaurant for pizza and then gave him a beautiful gift. A wonderfully extravagant gift. Some would call it ugly; more polite folks would stop with gaudy. But a good mother knows true style when she sees it. And a good mother knows that some gifts speak volumes. Even a blue denim, Western-cut shirt with purple pearl buttons. It was his graduation gift. Late. And certainly not in the family budget. But what does love care?

Two days later, David and his gaudy shirt walked into what would become our world for the next year.

As that first semester wound down, all thoughts turned to exams and to going home for Christmas. Especially going home for Christmas; exams were just the necessary hurdle everybody had to jump over before the trip home.

On that particular Christmas, we set about planning what would be known as the Thomas and Dave Christmas Invitational Christmas Party. Granted, we invited only Rick from the next room over, but every party has to have a theme. Knowing David's financial situation, Rick and I handled the entertainment and the refreshments, while David took care of the decorating.

The party was a great success. We watched *Frosty the Snowman* on a small black-and-white portable television, basking in the glow of our cedar tree trimmed with pull tabs from a semester's worth of Pepsi and Mountain Dew cans, a few ornaments from home, and a box of tinsel. And then we had a real feast: potato chips, chocolate chip cookies, bean dip, little smoked sausages, pickles, and Little Debbie Christmas Tree Cakes. Makes your mouth water just thinking about it.

David even wrapped a few boxes with paper from the art department and put them under the tree for effect. We ate, Frosty came to life, Rudolph saved Christmas, and all was right with the world (except for the bean dip part . . . bad idea). When the party ended, we all said our goodnights, went to our respective beds, and dreamed of home.

The next morning, Rick dropped in to say good-bye, and David presented him with a small package. To many people it would have looked like a regular old paperback science fiction novel. But to a science fiction fan who knew something of David's limited resources, it was a true gift indeed.

After much hugging, back slapping, and words of thanks, Rick headed home, and David and I resumed loading our cars. It was on my last trip upstairs to our dorm room that I saw the package on my bed. I was standing there looking at it when David walked in.

"What is that?" He asked the question and sat on the edge of his bed. I told him I didn't know. I just found it there.

"Well," he said, "Open it up. It could be a present."

"You think so?" I stripped off the wrapping paper and sat on my bed. There was a Christmas card in the box. And a handwritten note:

> Thomas, I can't begin to thank you enough for your friendship. This has been a tough semester, and you have been more than a friend. Thank you for listening. Thank you for everything.
> Merry Christmas,
> David

I pushed aside the tissue paper in the box and started to cry. My tears fell on a blue denim, Western-cut shirt with purple pearl buttons. The one his mother gave him.

I still have it. It has faded with age, and the wrinkles have become a permanent part of the fabric. And I pray the lesson it taught has become a permanent part of my fabric.

—*Thomas Smith*

The Beaded Bag

Mame, the mother of ten children, sat in the old rocker in the kitchen, her beaded bag in her lap. Hours before, she'd bathed the younger children and tucked them into bed, helped her husband candle and clean eggs to be sold the next morning, and churned a tub of butter. The smell of fresh bread baking in the oven pleased her. She sighed. After a busy day on the farm, these midnight hours were her own.

The clock chimed. Mame looked up at Lenora, her eldest daughter living at home, standing in the doorway. "Nora," she said, "I thought you'd be asleep, after helping with the milking and catching up on your studies."

Lenora smiled. "You know I can't sleep while you're still up."

"I know how that is." She strung three or four

shiny cobalt blue beads onto her needle and stitched them into place. "It's good to have company."

"The beading is taking a long time, Mama."

Mame laughed. "Can't work long before falling asleep," she said, smoothing her apron so she could see all the beads lying in her lap. "If I start to doze, read me some of that *Huck Finn* you're studying, will you? I always did favor Mark Twain."

"You and Daddy's sister, Aunt Vilate. Remember when I was nine, and she gave me *Tom Sawyer* for my birthday?"

Mame nodded. "Such a dear she is," Mame said, threading more beads. "Each year Vilate invites me to her luxurious home in Salt Lake City for a two-day stay. Old as we are, we still giggle like schoolgirls, reminiscing about those early days."

"She's like a sister, isn't she?"

"Oh, yes." Mame gazed wistfully at the pastel blues, greens, yellows, and violets in Vilate's floral painting hanging above the kitchen table. "She's an accomplished artist, you know. Paints like the masters." Mame paused. "But, even more important, Vilate has a kind heart that takes joy in making others happy." She pulled out the handkerchief tucked beneath her sleeve and wiped her eyes.

"Check the bread for me, will you please, Nora? I could use a hot heel of bread slathered with butter and honey."

"And a cold cup of milk?"

"Exactly."

Later, as her worn hands continued threading the shiny beads and working them onto the bag, Mame smiled as she remembered her last visit with Vilate.

"Come with me," Vilate had said, grabbing Mame's hand.

"Where are we going?"

"Downtown."

Mame caught her breath. "But I can't afford . . ."

Vilate hugged her hard. "Don't worry. You're my guest, and I've arranged for a special surprise!"

In the beauty parlor, the beautician coiffed Mame's beautiful dark auburn hair into a stylish do, a luxury indeed. A little while later, Mame's dark eyes sparkled as she caught her reflection in the department store mirror. What a gorgeous blue brocade dress! From the meager income of the Kimball farm, she knew she could never have had one so beautiful.

"You look regal, like a queen," Vilate said, circling Mame again and again. "Now for the final touch."

"The final touch?"

Vilate nodded. "A beaded bag will add that exquisite final touch to your new outfit," she said. "You choose the beads, and I'll show you how to make the bag."

The next day, with their heads together next to

Vilate's blazing fireplace, Mame had received her beading instructions.

Remembering, Mame smiled and sighed. *Wouldn't Vilate be surprised,* she thought, *if she knew that I was making the bag for her? If only I can finish it in time for Christmas.*

In and out, in and out went her needle, as the blue beads glimmered from the raised pattern on the bag. All was silent, except for the *tick, tick, tick* of the grandfather clock. Her eyes felt heavy.

"Mama?" Lenora tapped her on the shoulder. "You should go to bed. Here, I'll help you."

A month passed, then two, then three. Bouts of chicken pox worked their way through first one child, then the next, causing unimaginable worry and distress. Between baking soda baths to stop the itching and cool cloths to stop the fever, little time remained—not even in the midnight hours; yet, night after night, Mame worked on her beaded bag. Often, she and the rooster greeted the morning together.

"Goodness, Nora," Mame said one evening, "I never dreamed so many beads could fit onto one bag." She chuckled. "Well, I've hand-stitched the floral taffeta lining and made a pocket for the mirror." She handed Lenora the open bag. "What do you think? Shall I add a small ruffle around the top of the lining?"

"That would look smart," Lenora said. "Are you going to cover the mirror?"

"I thought I would—with a piece of matching taffeta."

"An elegant beaded bag for an elegant lady," Lenora said, hugging Mame.

"My thoughts exactly. But remember," Mame said, putting her finger to her lips and winking, "It's our secret."

Lenora grinned. "You'll get it done by Christmas, I know."

"I believe I will. After I finish the lining, I want to add seven rows of beaded tassels at the bottom."

"Wish I didn't have to leave for college next week," Lenora said, running her fingers over the tiny flowers carved in the silver frame at the top of the bag. "After all your work, I'd love to see the finished product."

"You'll see it on Christmas day, when Aunt Vilate comes for dinner." Mame kissed her daughter's cheek. "Thank you for your company and for keeping me awake."

In bed that night, Mame was awakened by a raspy sound, followed by a fit of coughing.

"Crozier, what is it?" she cried, raising her husband's head.

"C-c-can't . . . breathe . . . get . . . the doctor." He lay motionless in her arms, his face as white as death.

"Nora!" she screamed. "Come quickly! It's your father!"

Mame thumped his chest, rolled him over, massaged his back. He gasped. Rattling sounds escaped from his chest and seemed to catch in his throat.

"Call Doctor Whiting, Nora! Tell him to hurry!"

Mame helped Crozier to the overstuffed chair, covered him with an afghan, and sat beside him, holding his hand. An eternity seemed to pass before she heard the *chug, chug* of the doctor's car coming up the dirt driveway.

"Bronchial pneumonia," Dr. Whiting said. "Keep him warm and in bed. He's feverish. A shot of whiskey wouldn't hurt. If he gets worse, call me."

Despite her vigilant care, Crozier's condition did get worse.

"Maybe I should wait to start college, Mama," Lenora said. "You could use some help with the younger kids, and—"

"Your father and I won't hear of it," Mame interrupted. "The good Lord will give me the strength I need to bear this burden." She drew a cool bowl of water from the bathroom faucet and bathed Crozier's face. "Pack up your things, Nora. Your brother will be here to pick you up before you know it."

After Lenora left the room, Crozier wheezed, "Where are we going to get the money to pay for the rest of her tuition at Utah State?"

"The Lord will provide," Mame answered.

Later that evening, she finished the last remaining tassel on the beaded bag and held it up to the light. The beads glimmered and glistened. Mame hugged the bag to her chest as tears rolled down her cheeks.

"I know how much you would have loved it, Vilate," she said out loud. "It was to be my thanks to you for all you've done for me over the years. But Nora needs her education. I know you'd understand."

Sitting at the table, she wrote to her eldest son, Eddie:

> *Since your father has been ill, money has been scarce. Lenora has her college tuition for Utah State with the exception of fifteen dollars. Will you please take this beaded bag to the Catholic Carnival and have them raffle it off. Surely it is worth fifteen dollars!*
>
> *Love,*
> *Mother*

She tucked the note inside the bag, found a suitable box, and lovingly wrapped her gift in butcher paper. Tying it securely with string, she set the package on the table, where Reid would not forget to mail it on his way to school. In due time, the fifteen dollars arrived.

Three months later, Crozier had recovered and the family was celebrating Christmas. As Mame opened her special gift, tears fell upon the wrapping. She tried to speak, but no words came.

"We couldn't do it, Mama," Eddie said, wiping his eyes. "Nora told us about you, Aunt Vilate, and the beaded bag—how you worked on it night after night during the wee hours."

"All of us gave what we could," Reid explained, "even the younger ones."

Mame hugged each of her children in turn. "Thank you," she whispered to each of them. "Thank you."

That afternoon, Mame and her family watched as someone else's eyes filled with tears.

"Oh, Mame!" Vilate said, holding up the beaded bag. "This is my all-time favorite Christmas gift! How can I ever thank you?"

Mame's heart felt as though it would burst. Her eyes scanned the faces of her ten children, her dear husband, and her beloved Vilate. "You just did," she whispered.

—Mary Chandler

"The Beaded Bag" was first published in GRIT magazine, December 13, 1998.

 Christmas Is Delicious!

We were so excited and happy about taking our first trip to Radio City Music Hall with our son, Michael. The famous Christmas Spectacular was back in New York City, and it would be a wonderful experience for us all. My husband had never seen the show as a child, so it would be a first for the two men in my life. The weather was cold and crisp, and the city shone with holiday decorations and twinkling lights. Dressed in colorful red and green sweaters, we set off on our big adventure.

Our son's midtown Manhattan nursery school had planned a field trip for fifty of us, with our two- and three-year-olds in tow. We had purchased a block of tickets for the performance. Although I'd grown up in the city, I hadn't seen the Christmas show since I was ten years old. I looked forward to seeing the beautiful art deco building again, this time through the eyes of Michael, who had just turned three.

As we made our way to the theater, childhood memories flooded back to me. As the eldest of three daughters, my father chose me to accompany him on a yearly father-daughter "date" to Radio City. I could still remember parts of the Christmas show and my delight in going to an expensive seafood restaurant after the show with my dad. I hoped that Michael would remember this day and look back on it fondly as he grew up.

Michael was excited just to stand in line to get into the five o'clock show. He rarely saw the city by evening and was mesmerized by the traffic, the bright Christmas lights, and the crowd of children and adults. He kept up a steady stream of excited chatter throughout our wait.

"Where's Santa?" he asked.

"Are all these people Santa's helpers?"

Michael charmed everyone in line and proudly introduced us to the people standing in front and in back of us. In the contagious party-like atmosphere, we waited outside in the cold without complaint.

We made the requisite stop for snacks and souvenirs before going to our seats in the second mezzanine, having spent nearly the down payment on a house for five-dollar candy, five-dollar sodas, ten-dollar programs, and wildly expensive holiday novelties. Michael chose a stuffed Rudolph the Red-Nosed Reindeer as his special companion to hold during the show. The main lobby fairly vibrated with excitement, as children and parents rushed around making purchases before finding their places.

Our group spanned almost six rows of seats, and we were a noisy, overstimulated bunch of theater-goers. As the lights went down, handsome men and beautiful women skated onstage on a revolving set. We *oohed* and *aahed*. The colors! The costumes! The beauty of the holiday season and the telling of the Christmas story unfolded beneath us on the stage. All the while, Michael's classmates busily slid down from their seats to visit friends and to point out items of interest to all. I seemed to spend as much time relocating toddlers as I did watching the show.

Michael's eyes shone with joy and excitement. Before this, he had visited only a department store Santa, which had both thrilled and terrified him at the same time. Now, as the dancers came onstage, he grew more and more excited and pointed out everything that he saw to us. He commented on the characters and asked if he could go downstairs and touch the snowmen. I explained to him that this show did not include audience participation, as *Sesame Street Live* did. Still, he kept up his steady stream of happy toddler chatter, oblivious to the muted *Shssshs* lovingly directed toward him. Thank goodness we were in a child-friendly atmosphere, where his excited exclamations blended in with those of other children.

As the Nativity scene rolled onstage, Michael's eyes widened to the size of saucers. He asked us to tell him who the characters were, and I explained that they were Mary, Joseph, and the baby Jesus, along with the Wise Men and his favorite live animals: horses, cows, goats, and sheep. The love between parents and child were evident to Michael, and I kept my explanation simple, using words and descriptive phrases he could understand.

As soon as the words "baby Jesus" had left my mouth, Michael unexpectedly jumped up in his seat and shouted, "I love baby cheeses! And Swiss cheeses! And Bonbel and American cheeses, too!"

(At the time, we carried string cheese along with us wherever we went. Some children had security blankets; Michael had his cheese.)

Immediately after he shouted the words, nearby rows of parents broke into hysterical laughter. The superb acoustics of the hall amplified Michael's comments, and his exuberant voice traveled all the way down to the stage, as if he had spoken into a microphone. You could say that he stopped the show, for we noticed that Mary's and Joseph's shoulders were also shaking with silent laughter.

When I explained to Michael that it was "Jesus," not "cheeses," he was a bit disappointed. However, he quickly recovered, and said that he "loved baby Jesus and baby cheeses, too." Word of Michael's outburst had gone from tier to tier, all the way downstage. The show was stopped for almost five minutes, to allow everyone to recover and go on with the festivities. It took us much longer to regain our composure and settle down to enjoy the rest of the performance. Once I had clarified Michael's mistake, he sat happily, chewing on his beloved cheese, offering some to baby Jesus. "He looks hungry, too."

How simple, and yet rich, are the wonders and joys of childhood. In trying to create a Christmas memory for Michael, I'd forgotten that sometimes the best memories are unscripted and unplanned. And little could I have known that my three-year-old would inadvertently create a joyous moment for me and a whole theater of people. What a delicious, unforgettable way to commemorate this holiday season!

—*Robin E. Woods*

The Best Worst Christmas

Papa was going to town—all by himself! In those days, when you lived twenty miles from town and the top speed of your car was forty miles per hour, a trip to town was a major event and usually involved the whole family.

Each of us had important reasons to participate. Papa was the driver. Mama was in charge of the cream can and the egg crate, bartering cream and eggs for groceries. My brother, Bert, and I had to go because the barter agreement with the creamery included two Dixie cups, a small paper container of vanilla ice cream with a tiny wooden paddle for scooping. It was a wondrous treat, well worth the long ride to town and the hours waiting for the eggs and cream to be traded and the groceries to be purchased.

But on that December morning, Papa came up to the house right after milking, took a bath and shaved, and put on his best bib overalls, still stiff with starch. Then he went out to the Model A and drove away.

Bursting with indignation, Bert and I turned to Mama for an explanation. Mama was turning the handle of the cream separator and appeared not to notice that anything unusual had occurred. If she knew the reason for Papa's behavior, she wasn't telling.

Papa got back about four hours later. Apparently, the urgency of Mama's queries made them a little less discreet than usual. We overheard small scraps of conversation that we assembled later in our attic playroom: "something growing on the bone" . . . "can't fix it here" . . . "hospital in Minneapolis" . . . "don't cry" . . .

"Minny-apple-is?" The word was so long and unfamiliar, I struggled to pronounce it. "But how will he ever find it?"

"He'll use a map. Minneapolis is a very big place and it's on every map." Bert's bravado was intended for me, but it comforted us both.

Saturday, there was another trip to town. This time, we all went. Mama bought so many groceries there was hardly room for Bert and me to squeeze in between the flour sack and the boxes. We should have been pleased by the unusual plenitude, but there was something very disquieting about the change in routine.

When we came home from school on Monday,

Papa had already gone. Mama was punching down the bread dough with a fierce intensity.

"When's he coming back, Mama?" was as much as we dared ask.

"When they get the cancer out," said Mama. She had said the bad word, the one no one spoke when Uncle Ted got so sick that children couldn't visit.

After supper we lingered at the table to plan our schedules. Mama would do the milking. Bert would throw hay to the cows and to May and King, our gentle draft horses. And he would clean the stalls. I would pick the eggs and wash the dishes. Mama waited for Bert to complain about how early he would have to wake up to get all his chores done before school. Of course, had he, I would have interrupted with my opinion of the sour hen in the middle nest that always pecked at me. No one said a word.

"Well, then." Mama cleared her throat. "I suppose we had better get to it so we can get some sleep."

A week passed without word, then two. If we had more responsibility, we also had more privileges. No more wheedling and begging to listen to our favorite radio dramas. Mama let us have the radio on, even at the supper table. It took all the fun out of it. Some days, we were so worn out after our chores, we didn't even think about the *Lone Ranger* or *Sky King*.

Mama hardly spoke at all anymore. She sat in her rocking chair with her darning egg and an assortment of socks on her lap. If we looked at her, she would duck her head and peer intently at her stitches. We figured her eyes must be bothering her; they were red when she came out of her bedroom in the morning and they were still red when we came in from school in the afternoon and from our chores at night.

And Christmas was coming. Bert and I already knew it was going to be the worst Christmas ever. We had enough potatoes and side pork and home-canned vegetables to last for months, but the perishables purchased on our last trip to town were gone. We gazed with longing at the sack lunches of the more fortunate neighbor children: bananas, grapes, even store-bought bread with fancy bologna. We held our chokecherry jelly sandwiches carefully under our desks between nibbles. After lunch, the other children regaled us with descriptions of the wonderful toys to be found in the Sears Roebuck catalog. We already knew about them; we had a catalog, too. But the cream can and the egg crate hadn't moved from the basement since Papa had left, so we knew Mama's purse was empty.

"That stuff is for kids," Bert and I scoffed.

We decided that we would put our efforts into getting Mama through the holiday. We decorated the house with stars and bells cut from cereal boxes and silver canes fashioned from the pull strip of coffee cans. When school recessed for Christmas vacation, the teacher allowed us to bring the Christmas tree home. It didn't look quite the same after two weeks in the warm schoolroom and being dragged a mile down the dirt road, but it made the house smell nice.

Finally, it was Christmas Eve. Mama made *rommegrot* (a rich porridge made from pure cream), but there was no *lutefisk* (Swedish brined fish) that usually graced our holiday table. We had side pork with milk gravy, just like every other day. We hurried through the meal and then Bert and I coaxed Mama into the living room, intending to serenade her with all the Christmas carols we had learned for the school program. It didn't seem to be working. Halfway through "Silent Night," Mama excused herself and went to her room. We could hear her crying softly.

She hadn't exactly told us to go to bed, but we couldn't think of anything else to do, either. By the time it was dark, the house was silent.

It must have been near midnight when we were awakened by a bright light flashing on the bedroom wall. We knew what it meant: Someone was crossing the bridge by the schoolhouse. We rushed to the window and watched the car turn onto our road.

We burst into Mama's room. "Mama, Mama! There's a car coming down the ditch road."

But Mama was already up, reaching into the back of her closet, pulling out the black dress she never wore. "I saw the lights," she said.

Mama donned the black dress and silk stockings, and smoothed her hair into a bun. Then she seated herself on the sofa and folded her hands in her lap.

"Mama! They're coming here! We're getting company! Shouldn't we go outside and see who it is?"

"I know who it is," sighed Mama, "and they will find their way to the house."

It took that long for Bert and me to realize that company in the middle of the night was unlikely to be a good thing. We fell silent, studying Mama in her black dress, realizing what it meant. I started to wail, and Bert pulled me into the kitchen.

We watched as the car turned into the farmyard and drove all the way up to the house. There was a shuffling on the steps, but the expected knock never came. Instead, the door slowly opened and there stood Papa, his arms filled with packages.

Bert rushed to the living room. "Mama—come—please. Come—now," he stuttered.

Mama stopped in the doorway and gazed at Papa as if he were an apparition. He dropped the packages and swept her into his arms, kissing her right in front of us.

"I brought presents," said Papa.

"You are my present," whispered Mama.

—Doris Olson

An American
Christmas Story

This is our Christmas story, part of the spoken history of my family. It is an urban tale, a little brassy and rough around the edges. Maybe some grandmothers live over the river and through the woods, but mine did not. Perhaps yours didn't, either.

My maternal grandparents lived on Lagonda Avenue in Springfield, Ohio, an industrial town near Dayton. Their house was a two-story frame structure that crouched next to an alley in a neighborhood of aging houses, stores, and bars. Big semi trucks rumbled through all day and all night, because Lagonda Avenue was a state route, a major thruway in those days. As far back as I can remember, we went to my grandparents' for Christmas Eve. We always arrived early on the big night. My father and grandfather relaxed with highballs or tiny glasses of what they called "sipping whiskey" at the kitchen table, while my mother and grandmother applied finishing touches to supper.

My grandmother wore her usual spike heels and trousers, a Christmas apron tied securely around her middle, a corsage planted firmly on her ample bosom. Grandma was the center of the family universe, a woman with a steel backbone and a lap built for heavy use. My grandfather stayed in the background, in his flannel shirts and wire-rimmed spectacles. They had worked hard all their lives, both of them on rocky, played-out farms, my grandfather in iron furnaces and coal mines. After my grandfather retired, my grandmother took in renters and my grandfather worked as a security guard for one of the plants in town. Considering where they'd come from, where they were looked pretty good.

The house was festive, with spun glass snow and a crèche on top of the television set, and Christmas cards taped along the door frame. Electric candles burned in the front windows, the yellow flames staining the snow on the sills.

My brother and sister and I hovered around Grandma's shiny silver Christmas tree like moths about a flame. It had a spotlight with a colored plastic wheel that turned. The tree sparkled red, bleeding into gold, then green. We were always fascinated by the chameleon tree and by the mysterious packages piled underneath. Pajamas and clothes, for sure, but there was bound to be something from Aunt Doris, who lived in California and always seemed to know what kids liked. Maybe she'd sent *National Geographic* for my brother, who loved maps and faraway places.

As the evening wore on, the air fairly steamed with promise and impatience. We kids peered out the front windows and yanked open the door to the unheated sun porch. The Christmas Day turkey loomed in the chill semidarkness, snuggled in its roaster next to casseroles and custard pies. We paced to the front door, then back to the front windows. The watch for Aunt Hope had begun.

Hope was my mother's younger sister. She'd never had good luck with men, or maybe they'd never had good luck with her. In any event, she was the single mother of four sons by two different fathers. Hope worked at the International Harvester plant (a good union job, my grandfather said). Maybe she had to work late on Christmas Eve, or maybe it was hard to get four boys presentable. We didn't care. In the self-centered way of children, all we knew was that she was always late and that there would be no dinner and no presents until Aunt Hope arrived. When she finally did, powdered and per-fumed, dressed to the nines, sons in tow and carrying a shopping bag full of presents, Santa Claus himself couldn't have been greeted with more enthusiasm.

We welcomed our cousins with the shy reserve accorded those relatives seen mostly on holidays. We pulled extra chairs around the kitchen table, fighting over who got to sit on the step stool, and our Christmas Eve supper began. There were two kinds of meat, my grandfather's special potato salad, vegetables, relishes, mysterious home-canned condiments, and two kinds of pie. Because it was a special occasion, we kids were allowed to drink Coca-Cola with dinner.

Then we settled ourselves in the living room. My grandmother pulled the presents from under the tree, one by one, examined the tags, and passed them out to the rest of us. I remember one year I bought a set of cufflinks for my father (who never wore French cuffs), a quart bottle of lilac aftershave for my grandfather, and a red cut-glass ring for my grandmother (one size adjustable to fit all). Truly gifts of the Magi. All were accepted with great enthusiasm.

We passed around fudge and divinity sent by Aunt Beulah in Illinois. We sang carols in a rich chorus of related voices, "Away in a Manger" and "We Three Kings," and ending, as always, with "Silent Night." By the end of the evening, I was overwhelmed with prosperity and goodwill. As I struggled for sleep on the rollaway bed in the living room, I knew that nestled under my grandmother's silver tree were toilet water and dusting powder and a Tressy doll with hair that grows. My family slumbered around me, breathing softly while the semis thundered by outside.

Never since have I felt so wealthy.

I remember our last Christmas in Springfield. My grandmother lay confused in a nursing home, shrunken by pain and chemotherapy. She was propped up on pillows to help her breathe, her skin like aged parchment against the institutional sheets. My grandfather slumped awkwardly in the visitor's chair, trying to think of something to do with his work-roughened hands. When we arrived, Grandma brightened momentarily, greeting my sister and me.

"Well, hi, girls, where are those guitars?"

She'd always loved music, and we'd brought our guitars along to sing carols. By the time we were ready to play, she was lost again to that place she visited more and more often. The nurses suggested we sing in the lobby and they would send the music through the intercom into every room. We sang "Adeste Fidelis" and "Silent Night," tears painting our faces and dropping softly into our laps.

My grandparents are dead now, my parents also. Aunt Hope has loved and lost at least one or two more husbands. The color photographs we took on those long-ago Christmases have assumed the oddly brilliant hues typical of those times. They are snapshots, awkward, off-center, unedited—unlike my memories of those days. In my memories, my mother's face is rosy from an unaccustomed glass of wine. My grandmother presides over a groaning board, a choreographer of feasts. My father is broad-shouldered and strong again, singing tenor, the Chesterfields that killed him tucked safely in his shirt pocket. They are ghosts who come for the holidays, but they are friendly ones.

There are those whose Christmas memories are more traditional, more reverent, certainly more elegant. Never mind. This is our family's Christmas story, for what is a family but people who bring forward shared stories? My brother and sister and I still gather with our families on Christmas Eve. Children circle the tree and squirm restlessly through dinner. My sister checks the tags and passes out the presents. We sing carols in our related voices. And we keep candles in our windows for the ghosts.

—*Cinda Williams Chima*

The Best Lies Are for Christmas

"When does Santa die?" my four-and-a-half-year-old nephew, Jonathan, asked me.

"He's not going to," I said, watching him construct a Lego castle on his parents' back porch just outside Copenhagen on a humid July afternoon. We had landed on the subject because the holidays would be the next time we'd see each other.

"Why not? Mom says everybody dies."

"Well, Santa is not going to die, because he is magical."

He thought about this for a while, then, with all the skepticism of a little boy who listens to hip-hop, he asked, "How do you know?"

"I live next door to his cousin."

Jonathan knows that I live in America, a place he's never been to, but that might well be populated by the cousins of mythical figures, so he accepted my answer. All that aside, I'm entirely confident that Santa isn't going to die.

I remember asking my mother a similar question when I was very young. We had recently moved to a new neighborhood, and I was concerned that Santa might look for me in the wrong place. Perched on the kitchen counter with my legs dangling, I quizzed my mother while she poked a knitting needle into a batch of ginger and cinnamon cookies baking in the oven to see whether they were done.

She told me that all children are born with a tiny silver star in their head: Santa's navigation tool. That way, he never loses track of anyone. I believed her because in our family Christmas was rich with mystery and miracles. Every element was exciting, from gift shopping to the rolling of the seasonal rum balls.

The tree was particularly important. Growing up in Denmark, there was no shortage of conifers, but for us, it had to be the right kind. The magic kind. We would consider only noble firs or white spruces, because of their soft, fragrant needles, dark green with a silvery white tinge, and pleasing pyramid shape, kind of like a Victorian noblewoman's ball gown. Other families we knew would go for the tallest tree they could fit in the living room, but my mother knew the value of detail over volume, and because tall trees often have a gangly, adolescent look, our tree never stood higher than five feet. The decorations reflected the same philosophy. The ornaments had to be delicate, with a certain old-fashioned sweetness, like the vulnerable silver trumpet we had from my grandmother's time.

Each year around Christmas, schools would dedicate a day to making decorations for the tree and every kid in Denmark would glue together endless garlands of cheap multicolored paper. I did, too, but mine never went on the tree; instead, they joined heaps of other Christmas junk covering our walls and bookshelves all through the yuletide month: grinning cardboard Santas with cotton wool beards, yellow straw bucks with bows of red silk tied around their horns, and hundreds of paper doll *nisser*. Nisser are little old men with gray beards and red hats, mischievous elflike creatures believed to live in Danish people's attics, emerging at Christmas for bowls of oatmeal left out by kind folk.

Whatever else we put up around the house, the tree was sacred, and my mom and I spent black winter afternoons sipping mulled wine and cutting plum-colored silk paper into angels, stars, and plaited paper hearts. Every year, we saved the tree decoration ceremony for Christmas morning, December 24 in Denmark. We laid out all the ornaments on our massive oak dining table: indigo globes

and tiny silver bells, sugar hearts in miniature baskets, snowy swans with glass beads for eyes,
pinecones painted white and dusted with glitter,
Santa-shaped cakes with beards of icing. Then we
approached the naked tree like a couple of stylists
dressing a Hollywood celebrity.

"What do you think, *musling*," my mother asked,
stepping back to admire our efforts. (Her pet names
for me are all food-related. To this day, I'm a mussel
[musling], a sausage, a raisin, a cupcake.) "Is she a
beauty or what?"

When everything was in place, we dotted the
tree with white wax candles. In the evening, once it
was lit, our tree looked like a fairy queen, her dress
sparkling and shimmering from every angle, alive
with light.

I had friends whose mothers thought Christmas
was more work than it was worth. My mother
couldn't get enough. To her, it was a wondrous, abun-
dant playground where adults could be children
again.

My mother had been poor as a child—the kind of
poor that asks for stale bread in bakeries at the end
of the day and searches the lakeshore for carps
spilled by fishermen unloading their nets. Not sur-
prisingly, she became a scavenger in her adult life,
stockpiling useful things like food, clothes, bed linen,
and old crockery. She also became a nurturer and

protector of children's imaginations, a job she did so well that, at age eleven, while wise to the Santa Claus story, I still firmly believed in elves and was fuzzy about werewolves.

Last summer, facing my nephew's interrogation about Santa's life expectancy, it would have been against the rules to tell him the truth: that his grandmother will make sure the baton is being carried forward by my sister and me. She has raised us to be the next-generation guardians of children's dreams, and we're doing our best to live up to it. To make it easier, we have split the responsibility. My sister cooks the traditional Danish holiday meal—a double bill of duck and roast pork, followed by a rice pudding full of chopped-up almonds. And I gather Christmas tree decorations from all over the world and make up stories about the cast of Christmas.

That is how I know for sure that Santa won't die. My mother would never allow it.

—*Rikke Jorgensen*

Kevin's Saint

"Santa for Special Kids on tomorrow's broadcast. See you then."

The tag line caught my attention. I raised my head from my book and saw a picture of a waving Santa on the television screen as the news credits rolled by. My heart began to pound. Could this be the Santa I've been looking for?

I picked up the phone and called the station, "That Santa tomorrow, can he communicate with deaf children?" I asked.

Over the rumble of the newsroom, I heard, "Yes, he's a retired schoolteacher who signs. He won't release his name, but he's scheduled to be at the Memphis city mall tomorrow. We'll be picking up the story through our affiliate news station."

"Memphis? You mean Tennessee, not in Florida?"

"Yes. Can I help you with anything else?"

"No, thank you." I hung up, disappointed.

Just then Jessica came into the office. Her face changed seeing my expression. "What's wrong?"

"You know I love your son like a nephew, right?"

She smiled. "Of course. You're his favorite babysitter."

"Well, I'd like to take him to Tennessee tomorrow to the Memphis mall, where a Santa who knows sign language is scheduled to appear."

"It's really sweet of you to think of Kevin. But he's six. He doesn't need to visit Santa Claus anymore. And I'd rather instill in him the true meaning of Christmas, Jesus' birth, not just exchanging presents."

I pled my case, wanting her to know how much it would mean to Kevin. He'd never met a Santa who could understand him. Last year when we'd taken him to our local mall, he'd signed his name to the Santa.

"Yes, I'll bring you that," the Santa had replied.

Kevin had cried for hours. He decided Santa didn't give gifts to children who couldn't hear and speak. *That isn't good enough,* I thought, *not for Kevin.* He deserved a Santa who could relate.

"You really want to drive all that way just so he can tell him he wants a Pokemon?"

"Santa isn't just a man in a red suit," I explained. "He's the spirit of giving. He is Jesus' helper, spreading cheer to all the little girls and boys, even the deaf ones. For the first time, Kevin will believe that Santa knows who he is."

She nodded. "Well, all right, we'll go tonight. Bring a map and your camera."

"Of course!" I laughed.

Later in the evening, Kevin piled into the minivan, clutching his pillow.

His mother signed, "Don't you want to see Saint Nick?"

Kevin moved his fingers. "He doesn't like me unless I write."

"That's not true," his mother mouthed slowly.

Soon, Kevin snuggled in his backseat bed as mile after mile drifted by. Palm trees and scrub brush gave way to reddened clay. We drove until the air chilled and the land grew hilly.

When we arrived at the mall early the next afternoon, Jessica signed to her wide-eyed son, "We're here."

Wiggling in anticipation, he signed, "Do you think Santa cares that I came?"

I looked around at all the cars and knew enough to nod my head yes.

Kevin jumped out of the minivan and took his mother's hand and mine. Together we walked through the crowded walkways to the open courtyard. There, on top of a platform, was an older man with real gray hair. His stomach looked pillow-plumped, but there was no mistaking his outfit of red and white. He sat enthroned next to a sparkling, bedecked Christmas tree.

His mother gestured, "That's him, straight from the North Pole."

Kevin's face flushed with excitement at the whole Yule scene. He vaulted up the steps and stood in front of Santa. His mother and I scampered to catch up. By the time we got to Santa's chair, Kevin was signing, "I'm Kevin Johnson from Orlando, Florida."

"Hello, Kevin. You live near Disney World," Santa signed back. "You've been very good this year. What would you like for Christmas? A Pokemon?"

I knew that was probably what all the little boys had asked Santa for, but Kevin's eyes lit up as if Santa knew him personally.

"You're the real Santa," Kevin signed.

"Anything else?" the rosy-cheeked Santa asked.

Kevin quickly moved his hands to cross his chest.

Complying, Santa stretched out his arms to give him a giant hug. Tears came to my eyes as I raised my camera to capture the moment.

All children are special, I know that, but "special" children like Kevin sometimes get shortchanged on the simple joys of childhood. Truly that anonymous Santa in Memphis—a retired schoolteacher who gave his time and his heart to children who needed to communicate in their own way—embodied the spirit of giving.

—*Michele Wallace Campanelli*

Tell Your Story in the Next *Cup of Comfort*!

W e hope you have enjoyed A *Cup of Comfort for Christmas* and that you will share it with all the special people in your life.

You won't want to miss our next heartwarming volumes, A *Cup of Comfort for Courage* and A *Cup of Comfort for Teachers*. Look for these new books in your favorite bookstores soon!

We're brewing up lots of other *Cup of Comfort* books and *Cup of Comfort* cookbooks, each filled to the brim with true stories that will touch your heart and soothe your soul. The inspiring tales included in these collections are written by everyday men and women, and we would love to include one of your stories in an upcoming edition of A *Cup of Comfort*.

Do you have a powerful story about an experience that dramatically changed or enhanced your life? A compelling story that can stir our emotions, make us think, and bring us hope? An inspiring story that reveals lessons of humility within a vividly told tale? Tell us your story!

Each *Cup of Comfort* contributor will receive a monetary fee, author credit, and a complimentary copy of the book. Just e-mail your submission of 1,000 to 2,000 words (one story per e-mail; no attachments, please) to:

cupofcomfort@adamsmedia.com

Or, if e-mail is unavailable to you, send it to:

A Cup of Comfort
Adams Media Corporation
57 Littlefield Street
Avon, Massachusetts 02322

You can submit as many stories as you'd like, for whichever volumes you'd like. Make sure to include your name, address, and other contact information and indicate for which volume you'd like your story to be considered. We also welcome your suggestions or stories for new *Cup of Comfort* themes.

For more information, please visit our Web site: *www.cupofcomfort.com*.

We look forward to sharing many more soothing *Cups of Comfort* with you!

Contributors

Karen Ackland ("Christmas Bread Pudding") lives in Santa Cruz, California, with her husband, who always gives wonderful Christmas presents. Karen develops marketing materials for small businesses and technology companies. Her short stories and essays have appeared in a number of online and print publications, including *A Cup of Comfort Cookbook*.

Teresa Ambord ("A Christmas to Remember") lives in Anderson, California, with her teenage son and her best friend and faithful pooch, Annie. Freelance writing is a growing part of her life. She writes in many genres, but is happiest when writing humor pieces.

Susanna Anderjaska ("Silver Belles") grew up in Chicago, where Christmas meant snow, hot chocolate by a crackling fire, and warm mittens. Now, she lives and writes in Phoenix, Arizona, where Christmas is sunshine, ice tea, and bathing suits. She's learned that outer things don't matter; it's the love residing within each heart that counts.

Andria Anderson ("What Stocking for Mother?") has been a music teacher in Chicago for twenty-nine years. She and her husband share two grown sons, one almost-grown daughter, and the restoration of their 120-year-old Victorian house. Her novels are currently seeking a publisher, and her shorter writings have appeared in various books and on Web sites.

Helen E. Armstrong ("Love Needs Expression") originates from Milwaukee, Wisconsin, and taught high school English. Since relocating to the Colorado Springs area, she has been a reporter for a newspaper and co-led The Compassionate Friends, a support group for bereaved parents. Helen has been married for thirty-three years.

Christy Lanier-Attwood ("Where the Heart Is") resides in Austin, Texas, with her husband, Randy. Together, they have four wonderful children and a precious granddaughter. Christy is a realtor, but her lifelong passion is writing. She graduated with a degree in journalism from St. Edward's University and recently completed her first mystery novel.

Leisa Belleau ("Just a Little Extra") lives with her family in Newburgh, Indiana, a historic town on the Ohio River. Listed in *Who's Who Among American Teachers*, she is an instructor of writing and literature. She has published poetry, fiction, and nonfiction.

Mauverneen (Maureen) Blevins ("Oh! Christmas Tree") is a freelancer from the Chicago area. The mother of three daughters, she also enjoys travel and humor and is an award-winning photographer. Deciding to "Work like you don't need the money," she quit her day job and is pursuing her passions of both writing and photography.

Petrea Burchard ("Things") is an actor and writer living in Southern California's San Fernando Valley. Between theater performances and television guest appearances on programs such as "The Guardian," "Providence," and "Strong Medicine," Petrea works on scripts, articles, essays, and the second draft of a first novel.

Michele Wallace Campanelli ("Kevin's Saint") is a nine-time national bestselling author who has written more than twenty-five short story books and many novels, and whose work has also appeared in anthologies. Her personal editor is Fontaine M. Wallace.

Candace Carteen ("A Long Way from Anywhere") resides in Battle Ground, Washington. She's a stay-at-home mom, homeschool teacher, and published author. She and her husband, George Blakeslee, have an adopted son and hope to adopt a sister for him.

Mary Chandler ("Priceless, Timeless" and "The Beaded Bag") lives in Rancho, Santa Fe, California. Her work has been widely published in national magazines, anthologies, newspapers, literary journals, and on the Internet. She loves to travel (especially if opera is on the agenda), enjoys visiting with family and friends, and is never without a good book.

Cinda Williams Chima ("An American Christmas Story") changed college majors fifteen times, exiting with a degree in philosophy. Today, she is a dietitian who writes frequently on health and family issues. Married and the mother of two sons, she lives in Strongville, Ohio.

James Robert Daniels ("A Good Night's Dance) is a freelance writer from Seattle, Washington. His first short story, "The Cushmakers," appeared in the *Mason County Journal* in 1976. Publisher Henry Gay claimed that it was the only fiction ever printed on his editorial page. "A Good Night's Dance" was awarded a *ByLine Magazine* Honorable Mention.

Barbara L. David ("Simply Magic") lives in Cincinnati, Ohio, with her husband, Geoff, and their five children. She earned a Phi Beta Kappa key during her undergraduate studies and taught English, journalism, and film studies before becoming a stay-at-home mom. Barbara enjoys freelance writing in moments between helping with homework and changing diapers.

Ann Downs ("Love, Dad") is a fifth-grade teacher of language arts and creative writing in the Oakfield-Alabama school district, a rural western New York community that has always been her home.

Barbara Williams Emerson ("My Brothers' Keeper") has worked in higher education for more than thirty years and is president of Emerson Consultants, specializing in academic management, student affairs, and diversity. An author, activist, and international speaker, she holds advanced degrees from Columbia University. She is the executor of her late father, Hosea Williams's, estate.

Sarah Thomas Fazeli ("A Joyful Noise") makes her home in Southern California with her husband, Alex. She is an aspiring fiction and screenwriter, and holds an M.F.A. from the California Institute of the Arts. She is passionate about practicing and teaching yoga, meditation, and other mind-body techniques. She dedicates this story to her mother.

Kristl Volk Franklin ("The Story of the Christmas Angel") writes and publishes award-winning fiction and creative nonfiction in the psychological thriller and inspirational genres, and also writes and produces for the screen and stage. She lives in The Woodlands, Texas, with her husband, Lee.

Pat Gallant ("Toy Soldiers") is a fourth-generation native New Yorker and mother of a son. Awarded a New Century Writer's Award in 1999 and again in 2002, her writing has been published in *Saturday Evening Post, Writer's Digest, New Press Literary Quarterly,* and several anthologies.

Sylvia Bright-Green ("The Purfect Tree") has been writing for twenty-five years and has published more than 500 articles, columns, and stories in local and national publications. She has coauthored books, hosted a talk show, and taught at conferences and colleges in her home state of Wisconsin.

Shelley Divnich Haggert ("Kids, Casinos, and Christmas") is a freelance writer whose essays and articles have appeared in dozens of regional and national magazines. She lives in Windsor, Ontario, where she is the editor of *Windsor Parent Magazine* and is surrounded by her family.

Lynn R. Hartz ("Daddy's Red Sweater"), a retired psychotherapist, now writes full-time from her home in West Virginia. Her first novel, *And Time Stood Still*—the story of the midwife who delivered the Christ Child—will be released in the summer of 2003.

Rikke Jorgensen ("The Best Lies Are for Christmas") is a freelance writer who tries to make up only the best-quality fibs about Christmas. She lives in San Francisco.

Kathryn E. Livingston ("Christmas Cards from Winston") is a freelance writer living in Bergen County, New Jersey, with her family. The coauthor of *The Secret Life of the Dyslexic Child* and *Parenting Partners*, she has also published articles in national magazines and is currently (always) at work on a novel.

Patricia Lugo ("Christmas Angels"), originally from Erie, Pennsylvania, resides in a log cabin that she and her husband, Bob, built in Page Township, Minnesota. She considers raising her four children, all outstanding adults, to be her greatest achievement. This retired grandmother of four and former dogsled racer operated a sled dog gear manufacturing and mail-order business for twenty years.

Carole Moore ("Silent Night") is a former police officer who writes a newspaper column and lives with her husband, two children, and kitty cats on the North Carolina coast.

Doris Hays Northstrom ("A Child Shall Lead Them") finds inspiration from family, friends, and the mountains and sky of her home state of Washington, where she teaches creative writing at a community college. Sending words out into the world to celebrate life is her passion.

Janet Lynn Oakley ("The Christmas Well") is the education curator at Skagit County Historical Museum in LaConner, Washington. She has published school and museum curricula as well as articles in historical journals and popular magazines, completed four novels and a picture book, and enjoys a good family yarn.

Teresa Olive ("The Reluctant Caroler") is a homemaker, mother of five (ages nine to twenty-five), pastor's wife, piano teacher, and freelance writer. Her writing ministry includes numerous published articles and five children's Bible story books. She lives in western Washington, where she enjoys animals, gardening, and singing in the rain.

Doris Olson ("The Best Worst Christmas") is a retired executive residing in Red Wing, Minnesota. She fondly recalls her childhood in a Scandinavian farming community in northern Minnesota, where shared sacrifice added a rich texture to their bucolic lifestyle.

Carol Tokar Pavliska ("Star of Wonder") lives with her husband and four children on a farm in Floresville, Texas, where she writes a family humor column for the local newspaper. Raising and homeschooling her children is her primary occupation and focus.

Julie Clark Robinson ("Ho Ho Hold On!") was too engrossed in making gingerbread housing complexes to write a proper bio at press time. Let's just say that she's a Type A person who has published in a few magazines and anthologies, but that will never be quite enough for her. Her family puts up with her in Hudson, Ohio.

Tammy Ruggles ("Christmas Dinner, Christmas Spirit") lives in the small rural town of Tollesboro, Kentucky, and is the single mother of a teenage son. In 2001, she had to retire from her job as a social worker when she became legally blind, but is enjoying a second career as a freelance writer.

Elaine L. Schulte ("A Swahili Christmas") is the author of thirty-six novels and hundreds of articles and short stories for both adults and children. She has lived in Europe and traveled extensively, but her "Swahili Christmas" turned out to be the best vacation of her life. She and her husband, Frank, have two sons and two grandchildren.

Bluma Schwarz ("Pure and Simple") is a semiretired mental health counselor and freelance writer, residing in Florida. At age sixty-nine, she published her first story in

Iowa Woman. Her stories have since appeared in *Potpourri, Potomac Review, AIM,* other volumes of the *A Cup of Comfort* series, and elsewhere.

Junella Sell ("Our Special Box of Love") was born and raised in the Allegheny Mountains of Pennsylvania. As a young bride, she moved to Ohio, where she continues to live with her husband of fifty-one years, Denny. They have three children, Cindy, Gregory, and Christopher; eight grandchildren; and ten great-grandchildren. Two of their five children, Donetta and Randy, have gone home to the Lord.

Barbara Hazen Shaw ("Joey and the Christmas Tree Lot") is a junk sculptor, amateur astronomer, kayaker, and property manager in Eugene, Oregon. She loves to burst out of her routine and travel to exotic places; so far, she's explored fifty-one countries.

Alaina Smith ("Grandma and Grandpa and Karen") has a passion for writing. Her inspirational true stories have been published in anthologies, and she has completed a novel. She lives near Portland, Oregon, with her husband, Frank.

David Michael Smith ("Miracle in Georgetown") is a lifelong resident of Georgetown, Delaware, and is happily married to his wife, Geralynn. In his "day job," he works as a training curriculum developer for a major bank. He has published two books and contributed short stories to several others.

Thomas Smith ("Lessons from an Ugly Shirt") is an award-wining newspaper reporter, television producer, writer, and essayist. His writing appears in publications ranging from *Pulpit Digest* to *Haunts* magazine. Married to the woman who hung the moon, he divides his time between Raleigh and Surf City, North Carolina.

Pat Snyder ("Hanukkah Lights Bring Christmas Miracles") is a lawyer, writer, and mother of three, who lives in Columbus, Ohio, and writes a monthly humor column, "Balancing Act," about the light side of balancing family and work.

Mary Helen Straker ("King David") lives six months in Zanesville, Ohio, and six months in Bonita Springs, Florida. A graduate of DePauw University, she has worked for a Zanesville newspaper and *The Seattle Times*. She is the mother of four children and grandmother of six.

Patty Swyden Sullivan ("Christmas Present") lives in Overland Park, Kansas. She has been published in anthologies, newspapers, and magazines. Her daughter, Katie, is a remarkable woman who has excelled in college and continues to inspire her mother with fresh perspectives on life.

Julian Taber ("Is That All There Is?") is a retired clinical psychologist who specialized in addictive behavior and is a recognized authority on problem gambling. He writes nonfiction books and satirical novellas, and lives on Whidbey Island north of Seattle, Washington.

Rita Y. Toews ("Figure of Love") lives in East St. Paul, Manitoba, Canada, with her husband and obligatory writer's cat. She has authored two novels and three children's books, and is currently working on a historical novel.

Kenya Transtrum ("The Porch People") lives in Boise, Idaho, where, along with her husband of thirty-two years, she has raised their six children. She is the grandmother of eleven grandchildren, which brings her much pleasure. She enjoys reading, traveling, and scuba diving. She is an author and the acquisitions editor for a national publishing company.

Kathryn O. Umbarger ("The Last, Best Gift") discovered the joy of writing at age fifty and since then has earned thirty-seven writing awards. She has been published in fiction, essays, poetry, and allegory, but her passion is writing for children. She lives with her husband on the Snake River in southeastern Washington, where she enjoys grandchildren, camping, and kayaking.

Peggy Vincent ("That's Love"), a retired midwife who has "caught" more than 2,500 babies, is the author of *Baby Catcher: Chronicles of a Modern Midwife*, a memoir. She lives in California with her husband of thirty-seven years and her teenage son. Two adult children live nearby.

Donna Volkenannt ("Santa Wore Cowboy Boots") lives in St. Peters, Missouri, with Walter, her husband of thirty-five years. "Santa Wore Cowboy Boots" is dedicated to the memory of their beloved son, Walter Erik, whose love and laughter they miss every day.

Robin E. Woods ("Christmas Is Delicious!") is a former early childhood art, music, and movement teacher living in Montclair, New Jersey. A frequent contributor to parenting publications, she hopes that her writing, which chronicles the innocent and sometimes humorous impressions of her children, will someday thrill and embarrass them.

 # About the Editor

olleen Sell shares a big old Victorian house on a forty-acre lavender farm bordering the Cascade Mountains in Oregon with her husband, T.N. Trudeau, a carpenter who is renovating their dream home. The editor of more than sixty published books and the former editor-in-chief of two award-winning magazines, Colleen has also coauthored and ghostwritten several books and published hundreds of essays and articles. She writes fiction, screenplays, serious nonfiction, and creative nonfiction.

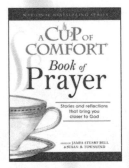